GOOD CLEAN JOKES FOR KIDS

BOB PHILLIPS

HARVEST HOUSE PUBLISHERS
Eugene, Oregon 97402

Illustrated by Sandy Silverthorne

GOOD CLEAN JOKES FOR KIDS

Copyright © 1991 by Harvest House Publishers
Eugene, Oregon 97402

Phillips, Bob, 1940-
    Good clean jokes for kids / Bob Phillips.
    Summary: A collection of jokes, grouped into such
categories as "Knock, Knock," "Crazy Thoughts," and
"Knee Slappers."
    ISBN 0-89081-902-5
    1. Wit and humor, Juvenile.   [1. Jokes.]
    I. Title.
PN6163.P49   1991   91-11146
818'.5402—dc20   CIP
                                         AC

Printed in the United States of America.

*This book is dedicated to all kids
(regardless of their age)
who love to smile...laugh...and even
groan at some of these crazy jokes.
It is also dedicated to many of my friends
whose names are in
this book at various spots.*

— ◆ —

*This book is best read
late at night when
you are* real tired.
Jokes are always *funnier then.*
*In fact, I had one friend who had
insomnia (trouble going to sleep).
He said that he read my book every night
and that it was better than a sleeping pill.
I had another friend who told me that
he really liked this new joke book.
He said that the pages were just
the size of his bird cage.
I told him that
was a fowl remark.*

About the Author

BOB PHILLIPS...is the author of over 20 books with sales reaching 3,000,000 copies in print. He is a California State Licensed Marriage, Family, and Child Counselor. He has received his BA from Biola University, his MA in Counseling from Cal State University in Fresno, and his Ph.D. in Counseling from Trinity Seminary. He is presently the Executive Director of Hume Lake Christian Camps, one of America's largest youth and adult camping programs.

Table of Contents

Flip & Flop

Flip: At what time of year is it best to use a trampoline?
Flop: What time?
Flip: In the springtime.

— ◆ —

Flip: What goes peck, peck, peck, bang?
Flop: I give up.
Flip: A chicken in a minefield.

— ◆ —

Flip: What is the difference between someone who writes songs and a corpse?
Flop: I have no idea.
Flip: One composes, and the other one decomposes.

— ◆ —

Flip: If a pig has a problem with pimples, what should you give it?
Flop: Who knows?
Flip: Oinkment.

Flip: Who rushes through the desert carrying a bedpan and dressed in white?

Flop: I don't have the foggiest.

Flip: Florence of Arabia.

— ♦ —

Flip: What is the best plan if two snails are having a fight?

Flop: You tell me.

Flip: I think I would just let them slug it out.

— ♦ —

Flip: If someone hits you in the head with an ax, what do you get?

Flop: I can't guess.

Flip: A splitting headache.

— ♦ —

Flip: What is the chiropodist's theme song?

Flop: My mind is a blank.

Flip: There's No Business Like Toe Business.

— ♦ —

Flip: What did the tiger say to his cub who was chasing a hunter around a tree?

Flop: I give up.

Flip: How many times have I told you not to play with your food!

Flip: Who rushes through the desert carrying a bedpan and dressed in white?
Flop: I don't have the foggiest.
Flip: Florence of Arabia.

Flip: What would you say to a cow that would give no milk?
Flop: That's a mystery.
Flip: I think you're an udder failure.

— ♦ —

Flip: What is the most favorite game at cannibal parties?
Flop: I'm a blank.
Flip: Swallow the leader.

— ♦ —

Flip: What do they call a short-legged tramp?
Flop: It's unknown to me.
Flip: A low-down bum.

— ♦ —

Flip: What is orange, covered with spots, and very deadly?
Flop: I'm in the dark.
Flip: A ladybug with a machine gun.

— ♦ —

Flip: If you crossed a parrot with a tiger what would you get?
Flop: I pass.
Flip: I don't know, but if it says "Pretty Polly," you had better smile.

Flip: What do they call a person who wears a one-button suit?

Flop: You've got me guessing.

Flip: A nudist.

— ♦ —

Flip: What is the best kind of bandage to put on someone who has had heart surgery?

Flop: How should I know?

Flip: Ticker tape.

— ♦ —

Flip: What do you call a man with a 2,000 pound safe on his head?

Flop: Search me.

Flip: Dead.

— ♦ —

Flip: What would be the difference between a counterfeit ten dollar bill and a crazy rabbit?

Flop: I have no clue.

Flip: One is bad money, and the other is a mad bunny.

— ♦ —

Flip: How can a knight tell what time of day it is by looking at his belly button?

Flop: I don't know.

Flip: That's easy. It is the middle of the night.

Knock, Knock

Knock, knock.
Who's there?
Who Who.
Who Who Who?
You sound like an owl.

Knock, knock.
Who's there?
Pasture.
Pasture who?
Pasture bedtime. You need your beauty sleep.

Knock, knock.
Who's there?
Passion.
Passion who?
Passion by and thought I'd see what's for dinner.

Knock, knock.
Who's there?
Osborn.
Osborn who?
Osborn today. When were you born?

Knock, knock.
Who's there?
Orange Juice.
Orange Juice who?
Orange juice going to let me come in?

— ◆ —

Knock, knock.
Who's there?
Opera.
Opera who?
Opera-tunity. You see, opportunity knocks more than once.

— ◆ —

Knock, knock.
Who's there?
Ocelot.
Ocelot who?
Ocelot of questions for a doorkeeper.

— ◆ —

Knock, knock.
Who's there?
Omar.
Omar who?
Omar goodness gracious! I must have knocked on the wrong door.

Knock, knock.
Who's there?
Ooze.
Ooze who?
Ooze the person in charge around here?

— ◆ —

Knock, knock.
Who's there?
Nana.
Nana who?
Nana your business.

— ◆ —

Knock, knock.
Who's there?
Willoughby.
Willoughby who?
Willoughby a monkey's uncle. I didn't think you were home.

— ◆ —

Knock, knock.
Who's there?
Wooden shoe.
Wooden shoe who?
Woodenshoe like to know who's knocking at your door?

Knock, knock.
Who's there?
Walter.
Walter who?
Walter-wall carpeting for sale. Would you like some?

— ◆ —

Knock, knock.
Who's there?
Weirdo.
Weirdo who?
Weirdo you think you're going?

— ◆ —

Knock, knock.
Who's there?
Wendy.
Wendy who?
Wendy wind blows, the cradle will rock...

— ◆ —

Knock, knock.
Who's there?
Value.
Value who?
Value be my Valentine? And value please let me in?

Knock, knock.
Who's there?
Viola.
Viola who?
Viola sudden you don't remember me?

— ◆ —

Knock, knock.
Who's there?
Uruguay.
Uruguay who?
You go Uruguay and I'll go mine.

— ◆ —

Knock, knock.
Who's there?
Usher.
Usher who?
Usher wish you would open the door and let me in.

— ◆ —

Knock, knock.
Who's there?
Uriah.
Uriah who?
Keep Uriah on the eye hole and you can see who is knocking.

Crazy Thoughts

Father: If I had seven bananas and gave you three, how many would you have left?

Son: I don't know.

Father: You don't know! Why not?

Son: At school we do all of our arithmetic in apples and oranges.

— ◆ —

School Principal: Excuse me, son. How do you like the beans we are serving at lunch today?

Student: I think that they are awfully hard, sir.

The principal picked up a spoon and dipped it into the student's beans and tasted them.

School Principal: They're not hard at all. They seem very soft to me.

Student: They should be now. I chewed those beans for ten minutes and put them back on my plate just before you came.

— ◆ —

Hunter: In Africa I used to chase the wild lions on horseback.

Listener: That's amazing. I didn't know that lions could ride horses.

Don: I failed every subject except biology.

Gerald: How did you keep from failing that?

Don: I didn't take biology.

— ♦ —

John: When I die, I'm going to leave my brain to science.

Ralph: Well that's good. Every little bit helps.

— ♦ —

Jeff: I know a hiker who went without sleep for ten days and wasn't the least bit tired.

Paul: That's impossible. How could that be?

Jeff: He slept at night.

— ♦ —

Mother: Jimmy, have you packed everything for our trip?

Jimmy: Yes, mother.

Mother: Did you pack your soap and toothbrush?

Jimmy: Soap and toothbrush! I thought this was supposed to be a vacation.

— ♦ —

Traveler: I would like a round trip airline ticket, please.

Agent: I'm sorry, but all of our tickets are rectangular in shape.

Ernie: I know a man who drove clear across the United States without knowing he had a flat tire.

Dave: I can't believe that's true.

Ernie: It's true. His spare tire in the trunk was flat.

— ◆ —

Ron: I always think it is best to write on a full stomach rather than an empty one. What do you think?

Lon: Actually, I think that it is much better to write on paper.

— ◆ —

Gerald: My son had twins and named both of the boys Ed.

Don: That's strange. Why did he do that?

Gerald: I guess that he thought that two Eds were better than one.

— ◆ —

Did you see the latest sign in the church nursery? It said: All babies are subject to change without notice.

— ◆ —

Johnny: If I had a face like yours, I'd put it on a wall and throw a brick at it.

Robbie: If I had a face like yours, I'd put it on a brick and throw a wall at it.

Husband: I was really great in sports when I was younger. I had the great body of an athlete.

Wife: Well, you still have the feet.

— ◆ —

On the way to the water hole a snake met seven zebras and four giraffes. Each giraffe had a bird sitting on its head, and there were three gorillas sitting on the back of each of the zebras. How many animals were going to the water hole?

Only the snake. The rest of the animals were coming back from the water hole.

— ◆ —

Did you hear about the kamikaze pilot who had trouble with indecision?

He flew 105 missions.

— ◆ —

Bill: How can you drop an egg four feet onto a concrete sidewalk without breaking it?

Jill: I give up. How?

Bill: Drop it from five feet.

— ◆ —

Carl: If a horse is tied to a 20-foot rope, how can it reach a pile of hay that is 40 feet away?

Gary: I give up. How?

Carl: The rope is not tied to anything.

Teacher: If a man is in a jail cell with no doors and no windows... and there are no holes in the ceiling or trapdoors in the floor... and yet when the guard comes in the morning, he finds that the prisoner has escaped... how did he get out?

Student: Through the doorway. There were no doors, remember?

— ♦ —

Larry: You still owe me a dollar for that honey.
Mary: What honey?
Larry: I didn't know you cared!

Ned & Ted

Ned: What did the large insect say to the small insect?
Ted: Stop bugging me.

— ♦ —

Ned: What is big and purple and eats rocks?
Ted: A big purple rock eater.

— ♦ —

Ned: If you cross a clock with a chicken, what do you get?
Ted: I have no clue.
Ned: An alarm cluck.

Ned: How is the moon held up?
Ted: With moonbeams, I think.

— ◆ —

Ned: What is smooth, yellow, and tastes good, but is very dangerous?
Ted: I don't know.
Ned: Shark-infested custard.

— ◆ —

Ned: What is a doughnut?
Ted: Beats me.
Ned: Someone who is crazy about money.

— ◆ —

Ned: Albert Einstein told what kind of jokes?
Ted: I can't guess.
Ned: Wisecracks.

— ◆ —

Ned: What is the definition of a ringleader?
Ted: I have no idea.
Ned: The first person in the bathtub.

— ◆ —

Ned: Name a famous book written about cats.
Ted: What can it be?
Ned: A Tale of Two Kitties.

Ned: What do you get if you cross a skunk and a bear?

Ted: You tell me.

Ned: Winnie-the-Phew.

— ◆ —

Ned: What is the favorite thing for frogs to sit on?

Ted: Who knows?

Ned: Toadstools.

— ◆ —

Ned: What teaches school, is green, and is wet all the time?

Ted: You've got me.

Ned: The Teacher from the Black Lagoon.

— ◆ —

Ned: On a hot day what is the best kind of letter to read?

Ted: My mind is a blank.

Ned: Fan mail.

— ◆ —

Ned: What is the most selfish pig on the highway called?

Ted: I don't have the foggiest.

Ned: A road hog.

Ned: What did the tire jack say to the car?
Ted: It's unknown to me.
Ned: Can I give you a lift?

— ♦ —

Ned: What is the politest thing to say when you are introduced to a road?
Ted: I'm in the dark.
Ned: Hi, way!

— ♦ —

Ned: What did one car muffler say to the other car muffler?
Ted: Search me.
Ned: Boy, am I exhausted!

— ♦ —

Ned: If you crossed a frog and a rabbit what would you get?
Ted: You've got me guessing.
Ned: A bunny ribbit.

— ♦ —

Ned: What would be worse than seeing the fin of a shark while you were swimming in the ocean?
Ted: How should I know?
Ned: Seeing its tonsils.

Tongue Twisters

Say the following phrases three times . . . real fast.

Shoot silly sheep if you like sheep soup.

— ♦ —

Cheap chunky chop suey.

— ♦ —

Silly shapeless sashes sag sadly.

— ♦ —

The sick sheriff sought six sick sardines.

— ♦ —

Take the cheap silly ship trip.

— ♦ —

Zelda sews zither covers.

— ♦ —

Cease sitting on slippery snakes in the salty seething sea.

— ♦ —

The chief chef sits in the cheap seat section.

Sally saves six Swiss wrist Swatch watches.

— ♦ —

Shocked Susie slid slowly on seven slippery snakes.

— ♦ —

Unique New York.

— ♦ —

Thin single shingles, thin tin thimbles.

— ♦ —

Six chicks lick sticky licorice.

— ♦ —

Sally sells sick snails smelling salts.

— ♦ —

Smart short soldiers should shoot sharks safely.

Bob & Ken

Bob: What did the father buffalo say when his son went to Disneyland?

Ken: I have no clue.

Bob: Bison!

Bob: What is the side dish that spiders eat with their hamburgers?

Ken: I don't know.

Bob: French flies.

— ◆ —

Bob: What do you call a 300-hundred pound football player with a bad temper?

Ken: Beats me.

Bob: Sir!

— ◆ —

Bob: What does the funniest boy at school eat for breakfast?

Ken: I can't guess.

Bob: Cream of Wit.

— ◆ —

Bob: What does the Spanish bullfighter say to his chickens?

Ken: I have no idea.

Bob: Oh, lay!

— ◆ —

Bob: What is the favorite course of snakes who go to school?

Ken: You tell me.

Bob: Hisss-tory.

Bob: What is the name of the smartest tree in the forest?

Ken: I give up.

Bob: Albert Pinestein.

— ◆ —

Bob: What song do you usually hear bees singing?

Ken: Who knows?

Bob: Stinging in the Rain.

— ◆ —

Bob: What do you get if you cross an elephant and a skunk?

Ken: You've got me.

Bob: A very big stink.

— ◆ —

Bob: What can you hold in your right hand but not in your left hand?

Ken: I'm in the dark.

Bob: Your left elbow.

— ◆ —

Bob: What has no length, width, or thickness, but still can be measured?

Ken: It's unknown to me.

Bob: The temperature.

Bob: What is big and gray and wears a mask?
Ken: I don't have the foggiest.
Bob: The Elephantom of the Opera.

— ◆ —

Bob: What did one pig say to the other pig?
Ken: Search me.
Bob: Let's be pen pals.

— ◆ —

Bob: What do you call a deer that is blind?
Ken: My mind is a blank.
Bob: No-eye-deer.

— ◆ —

Bob: What is green, has a guitar, and sings?
Ken: You've got me guessing.
Bob: Elvis Parsley.

— ◆ —

Bob: What is a ten-letter word that begins with g-a-s?
Ken: Beats me.
Bob: Automobile.

— ◆ —

Bob: What do they call a very selfish girl?
Ken: How should I know?
Bob: Mimi.

Bob: If your dog chews up your favorite book, what should you do?

Ken: I pass.

Bob: Take the words right out of his mouth.

— ♦ —

Bob: Guess what happened when my father ran away with the circus?

Ken: I have no clue.

Bob: The police made him bring it back.

— ♦ —

Bob: What word if pronounced right is wrong but if pronounced wrong is right?

Ken: I don't know.

Bob: Wrong.

The Answer Man

Q: Who is the only person in baseball to play for every game?

A: The organist.

— ♦ —

Q: Who was the man at the door with a drum in his hand?

A: I don't know, so I told him to beat it.

Bob: If your dog chews up your favorite book, what should you do?

Ken: I pass.

Bob: Take the words right out of his mouth.

Q: Who was the heaviest Indian in the wild West?
A: Ton-to.

— ♦ —

Q: Who invented spaghetti?
A: It must have been someone who used his noodle.

— ♦ —

Q: Who is radioactive and wears a mask?
A: The Glowin' Ranger.

— ♦ —

Q: In prehistoric times, what was the scariest dinosaur called?
A: The Terror-dactyl.

— ♦ —

Q: Who was the girl in the story that put her foot into a glass slipper . . . and in the process, smashed it to pieces?
A: Cinder-elephant.

— ♦ —

Q: What do you call a person who always has friends over for dinner?
A: A cannibal.

Q: What do they call a person who is angry and drives away all of his customers?

A: A taxicrab driver.

— ♦ —

Q: Who makes fine clothes, alters suits, and eats spinach all the time?

A: Popeye the Tailorman.

— ♦ —

Q: What do they call a person who earns a living without doing a day's work?

A: A night watchman.

— ♦ —

Q: What do they call a driver who can never be arrested by the police for speeding?

A: A screwdriver.

Rib Ticklers

Nancy: Who is at the door?
Cathy: The Invisible Man.
Nancy: Tell him I can't see him.

— ♦ —

Old Grouch: Give me two pounds of dog food now!
Salesclerk: Certainly, sir. Shall I wrap it up or will you eat it here?

A very shy young man went to buy a new pair of spectacles. Behind the counter was a very pretty girl. The young man became very flustered by her good looks and said:

"I—I would like a pair of rim-specked hornicles... I—I mean, I want a pair of heck-rimmed spornicles... I—I mean..."

At this point the girl became flustered by the handsome young man and said:

"I know what you are looking for. You want some rim-sporned hectacles."

— ◆ —

Husband: I wonder where I got that flat tire.
Wife: You probably got it in that last fork in the road.

— ◆ —

She: Would you like to come to my party next Friday?
He: I sure would. Where do you live?
She: I live at 2833 Ginger Lane. Just press the buzzer with your elbow.
He: Can't I just press the buzzer with my finger?
She: Well, you're not coming empty-handed, are you?

— ◆ —

Customer: I would like to buy a mirror.
Salesclerk: Would you like a hand mirror?
Customer: No, I want to see my face not my hand.

City Slicker: Why do you have two barrels on your shotgun?

Hunter: In case I miss the bird with the first shot, I can get him with the second shot.

City Slicker: Why don't you fire the second shot first?

— ◆ —

Store Manager: I saw you arguing with that customer who just left. I told you before that the customer is always right. Do you understand me!

Salesclerk: Yes, sir. The customer is always right.

Store Manager: That's better. Now what were you arguing with the customer about?

Salesclerk: Well, sir, he said you were an idiot.

— ◆ —

A man who ran out of gas on a country road finally came across a farmer in the field near the road.

"How far is it to the nearest gas station?" the man asked.

"About ten miles as the crow flies." replied the farmer.

"And how far would it be if it walked?" asked the man.

— ◆ —

Daughter: I've just made the turkey soup.

Father: Thank goodness for that. I thought it was for us.

George: Yesterday I saw a man fall from a 30-foot ladder.

Dwight: Was he hurt badly?

George: Not a bit. He fell off the bottom rung.

— ♦ —

Bill: I hear you went to Newport Beach.

Jill: Yes, I went to see the sea.

Bill: Well, did the sea see you?

Jill: Yes, it did.

Bill: How do you know?

Jill: It waved at me.

— ♦ —

Julie: Mom, can I have two pieces of cake, please? Please?

Mother: Certainly. Take this piece of cake and cut it in two.

— ♦ —

For Sale: Pedigree Doberman. Eats anything. Fond of children.

— ♦ —

Father: My son has been practicing the guitar for three years.

Friend: Well, is he any good?

Father: No. It was two and a half years before he found out he wasn't supposed to blow it.

Customer: Three pounds of kiddles, please.

Butcher: You mean three pounds of kidneys, don't you?

Customer: That's what I said, diddle I?

— ◆ —

I don't want to say that I live in a small apartment, but I had to scrape off the wallpaper in order to get the furniture in.

— ◆ —

Mary: Who takes after his father?

Larry: A thief's son.

— ◆ —

A man was driving down the freeway when all of a sudden he looked out his right window and saw a man on a bicycle, pedaling furiously as he passed him. The driver of the car stepped on the gas and went faster and passed the man on the bicycle. In just a moment, the man on the bicycle passed the car again. This time the driver of the car went even faster. Again the man on the bicycle passed the car.

Finally the driver of the car stopped. The man on the bicycle stopped by the right window. The driver of the car rolled down the window.

"Thank goodness you've stopped," said the man on the bicycle. "I had my suspenders caught in your back bumper."

Peggy: I bet I can make you say purple.

Ken: I bet you can't.

Peggy: What are the colors of the flag?

Ken: Red, white, and blue.

Peggy: There you are. I told you I could make you say blue.

Ken: You lose. You said you could make me say purple.

Peggy: And you did.

Nit & Wit

Nit: If you try to cross a lake in a leaky boat, what do you get?

Wit: I have no clue.

Nit: About halfway.

— ◆ —

Nit: What lives at the bottom of the sea, is brightly colored, and is popular around Easter?

Wit: I don't know.

Nit: An oyster egg.

— ◆ —

Nit: If a lawyer was hurt in a swimming pool, what kind of court case would he bring?

Wit: Beats me.

Nit: A bathing suit.

Nit: What two things are impossible to have for dinner?

Wit: I can't guess.

Nit: Breakfast and lunch.

— ◆ —

Nit: What is normal sight for a monster?

Wit: I have no idea.

Nit: 20-20-20-20-20.

— ◆ —

Nit: What event do buffaloes celebrate every 200 years?

Wit: You tell me.

Nit: The Bison-tennial.

— ◆ —

Nit: What goes "Thump, thump, thump, slosh"?

Wit: I give up.

Nit: An elephant with one wet sneaker.

— ◆ —

Nit: What was Samuel Clemens' pen name?

Wit: I didn't know he had a name for his pen.

— ◆ —

Nit: What room in the house do all ghosts stay out of?

Wit: You've got me.

Nit: The living room.

Nit: What do you call a huge whale with a large vocabulary?
Wit: That's a mystery.
Nit: Moby Dick-tionary.

— ◆ —

Nit: When chickens become ghosts, what sound do they make?
Wit: I'm blank.
Nit: Peck-a-boo.

— ◆ —

Nit: What movie channel should you watch with a can of air freshener handy?
Wit: I don't have the foggiest.
Nit: H-BO.

— ◆ —

Nit: What is the name of the famous cartoon maker who lived in a safe?
Wit: It's unknown to me.
Nit: Vault Disney.

— ◆ —

Nit: What is the name for a knight who is caught in a very bad windstorm?
Wit: I'm in the dark.
Nit: Nightingale.

Nit: What do they call a Santa Claus who drops the presents all the time?

Wit: Search me.

Nit: Santa Klutz.

— ♦ —

Nit: What is the most popular game show for fish?

Wit: You've got me guessing.

Nit: Name That Tuna.

— ♦ —

Nit: Where is the largest diamond in the world found?

Wit: I pass.

Nit: On a baseball field.

— ♦ —

Nit: Does it take longer to run from first base to second base or from second base to third base?

Wit: How should I know?

Nit: It takes longer to run from second base to third base because there is a shortstop in the middle.

— ♦ —

Nit: What do they call it when pigs do their laundry?

Wit: I don't know.

Nit: Hogwash.

When, When, When

Q: When does society say it is okay to belt your children?
A: When they get into the car.

— ♦ —

Q: When a girl slips and falls while roller skating, why can't her brother help her up?
A: He can't be a brother and assist her, too.

— ♦ —

Q: When a lemon calls for help, what does it want?
A: Lemonade.

— ♦ —

Q: When is the best time to lose your temper?
A: When you have a bad one.

— ♦ —

Q: When are people very glad to be down-and-out?
A: After a bumpy plane trip.

Rich & Dave

Rich: What is big, famous, and spouts water?
Dave: I have no clue.
Rich: The Prince of Whales.

Rich: What is the most famous fish in Hollywood?
Dave: I don't know.
Rich: The starfish.

— ◆ —

Rich: What kind of cow eats with its tail?
Dave: I give up.
Rich: They all do. Cows do not remove their tails to eat.

— ◆ —

Rich: What do you get if you cross an elephant and a parrot?
Dave: I can't guess.
Rich: Something that tells everything it remembers.

— ◆ —

Rich: Do you know what happened to the Italian glassblower?
Dave: I have no idea.
Rich: He inhaled and got a pane in his stomach.

— ◆ —

Rich: What do you get if you cross a banjo with a chicken?
Dave: You tell me.
Rich: You get a self-plucking chicken.

Rich: What is green and always points north?
Dave: Beats me.
Rich: A magnetic pickle.

— ◆ —

Rich: What wears a mask, smells good, and rides a horse?
Dave: Who knows?
Rich: The Cologne Ranger.

— ◆ —

Rich: What did the cow say when it finished eating a bale of hay?
Dave: You've got me.
Rich: Well, that's the last straw.

— ◆ —

Rich: What is the worst thing to say to an airline pilot?
Dave: My mind's a blank.
Rich: Hi, Jack!

— ◆ —

Rich: What sits on the bottom of the sea with a lot of gold and shakes?
Dave: I don't have the foggiest.
Rich: A nervous wreck.

Rich: What is the best way to hunt bear?
Dave: It's unknown to me.
Rich: Take off your clothes.

— ♦ —

Rich: What would happen if an insane goat fell into a blender?
Dave: I'm in the dark.
Rich: You would have a crazy mixed-up kid.

— ♦ —

Rich: What do they call a skeleton that will not get out of bed?
Dave: Search me.
Rich: Lazy Bones.

— ♦ —

Rich: What five-letter word has six left when you take away two letters.
Dave: How should I know?
Rich: Sixty.

— ♦ —

Rich: If you get a sunburn on your stomach, what is it called?
Dave: I pass.
Rich: Pot roast.

Rich: What kind of house weighs the least?
Dave: You've got me guessing.
Rich: A lighthouse, of course.

— ◆ —

Rich: What should you say when you meet a person with two heads?
Dave: I have no clue.
Rich: Hello, hello!

— ◆ —

Rich: What do they call a person who looks over your shoulder while you are eating at the lunch counter?
Dave: I don't know.
Rich: A counterspy.

— ◆ —

Rich: What do you get if you cross a cocker spaniel, a poodle, and a rooster?
Dave: Beats me.
Rich: A cockapoodledoo.

— ◆ —

Rich: What would happen to Ray if he were to jump off of the Brooklyn Bridge?
Dave: I can't guess.
Rich: They would call him X-Ray.

The Answer Man

Q: How can you double your money quick?
A: Fold it over and put it into your pocket.

— ◆ —

Q: Do hot dogs speak the truth?
A: Yes, they speak quite frankly.

— ◆ —

Q: How can you tell if there has been a hippopotamus in your refrigerator?
A: You can see his footprints in the butter.

— ◆ —

Q: What is the fastest way to get rich by eating?
A: Eat fortune cookies.

— ◆ —

Q: How do you make a hamburger roll?
A: You take it to the top of a very steep hill and give it a push.

— ◆ —

Q: What is the best way to take care of a very sick pig?
A: Take it to the hospital in a hambulance.

Q: What is the best way to run over an elephant?
A: Climb up its tail, make a mad dash to its head, and then slide down its trunk to the ground.

— ♦ —

Q: How many pairs of shoes can you put into an empty closet?
A: Just one...after that it isn't empty!

— ♦ —

Q: What is the easiest way to tell the difference between a hen and a rooster?
A: Toss some corn on the ground. If he eats it, it's a rooster; if she eats it, it's a hen.

— ♦ —

Q: What is the fastest way to remove varnish?
A: Take away the letter R.

— ♦ —

Q: How do you fit six elephants into a car?
A: Put two in the back seat, two in the front seat, one in the glove box, and one in the trunk.

— ♦ —

Q: Is it possible to knock over a full glass without spilling any water?
A: Yes. Fill the glass full of pop.

Q: How do you fit six elephants into a car?
A: Put two in the back seat, two in the front seat, one in the glove box, and one in the trunk.

Q: Is it possible to get out of a locked room with only a piano in it?
A: Yes, it is. Play the piano until you find the right key and then unlock the door.

— ◆ —

Q: What is the best way to keep an elephant from slipping through the eye of a needle?
A: Tie a knot in its tail.

— ◆ —

Q: If you are lost in the desert and do not have any food, what is the best way to avoid starvation?
A: Eat the sand-which is there.

— ◆ —

Q: How does a hippopotamus get down out of a tree?
A: He sits on a leaf and waits for autumn.

— ◆ —

Q: What do people from the South usually drink water out of?
A: Dixie cups.

— ◆ —

Q: How fast can you drive on roads in Egypt?
A: Sixty Niles an hour.

Q: How do you keep a person from sleepwalking?
A: Spread tacks all over the floor.

— ♦ —

Q: How can you tell you are in bed with an anteater?
A: He has an "A" on his pajamas.

— ♦ —

Q: How many feet are there in a pasture that is filled with 200 cows, 40 sheep, 7 dogs, 11 donkeys, and a farmer?
A: Two. All the rest are hooves and paws.

— ♦ —

Q: Is it possible to say rabbit without using the letter R?
A: Yes. Bunny.

— ♦ —

Q: How many seconds are there in a year?
A: Only 12. The second of January, the second of February, the second of March...

— ♦ —

Q: When farmers want to start a race, what do they say?
A: Ready, set...hoe!

Q: How many acorns usually grow on an average-size pine tree?

A: None. There are no acorns on pine trees.

— ♦ —

Q: Is it possible to name the capital of every state in the Union in less than 15 seconds?

A: Yes. Washington, D.C.

Silly Dillies

Son: Dad, what is the difference between Father's Day and Mother's Day?

Father: They're about the same, except you don't spend as much on Father's Day as on Mother's Day.

— ♦ —

Carla: I could marry anyone I please.

Marla: So, why haven't you gotten married?

Carla: I haven't pleased anyone yet.

— ♦ —

Theatrical Agent: And what sort of act do you do?

Applicant: I do bird impressions.

Theatrical Agent: I'm sorry, but that will not do. We have no job for you. I've got seven people who do bird impressions already.

Applicant: Okay, if you say so. *As the man got up and flew out the window.*

Ryan: Have you ever seen a square dance?
Lisa: No, but I've seen a salad bowl.

— ♦ —

New Wife: How do you like my sponge cake, dear?
Husband: It's a bit tough, honey.
New Wife: How can that be? I went to the store and bought a fresh sponge this morning.

— ♦ —

Client: There is only one way to make honest money.
Lawyer: What's that?
Client: I thought you wouldn't know.

— ♦ —

Fred: Do you need much training to be a garbage collector?
Frank: Not really. You just pick it up as you go along.

— ♦ —

Manager: So, you would like to have a job and work for our company, would you. What is your name?
Boy: Dick Tracy, sir.
Manager: Dick Tracy! My, my. That's a very well-known name, isn't it?
Boy: It should be. I've been delivering papers around here for years.

Bart: Why did you leave your last job?
Art: The manager accused me of stealing $25.
Bart: Didn't you make him prove it?
Art: He did.

— ◆ —

Boss: What's your name? I haven't seen you before.
Boy: Richard J. Hanson.
Boss: Say "sir" when you address me!
Boy: All right. Sir Richard J. Hanson.

— ◆ —

Phone Caller: Is it possible to speak to Don West?
Manager: Who is this speaking?
Phone Caller: This is Don's grandfather.
Manager: I am afraid that Don is not here right now. He's attending your funeral!

— ◆ —

Lady: Don't you just love the sound of those church bells?
Man: What did you say?
Lady: I said, don't you like the church bells that are ringing?
Man: What?
Lady: AREN'T THE BELLS A WONDERFUL SOUND?
Man: It's no use. I can't hear a word you're saying over those crazy church bells.

I have a friend who is very sentimental around Christmas time. Each year he takes off his socks and stands them up by the fireplace.

— ♦ —

Little Girl: I just banged my fumb in the door.
Teacher: Not "fumb," Christy. It's pronounced "thumb."
Little Girl: Yes, teacher. And I also banged my thinger as well.

— ♦ —

Policeman: Where are your taillights, mister?
Motorist: Never mind my taillights. Where's my trailer?

— ♦ —

Student: Is there any difference between a pound of feathers and a pound of lead?
Teacher: Absolutely not. There is no difference. They each weigh a pound.
Student: I bet there is a difference.
Teacher: That's impossible.
Student: Well then, could I drop a pound of feathers on your left foot, and a pound of lead on your right foot, and test your theory out?

— ♦ —

Customer: I want a hair cut! And I want it right now!
Barber: Yes, sir. Which hair would you like cut?

Ben & Len

Ben: What's green, stands in the corner, and has bumps?
Len: I have no clue.
Ben: A naughty pickle.

— ◆ —

Ben: What do frogs like to drink?
Len: I don't know.
Ben: Croaka-Cola.

— ◆ —

Ben: What do they call a lazy rooster?
Len: Beats me.
Ben: A cockle-doodle don't.

— ◆ —

Ben: What made the turkey dance?
Len: I can't guess.
Ben: It saw the fox trot.

— ◆ —

Ben: What cracks jokes all the time and is covered with feathers?
Len: I have no idea.
Ben: A comedi-hen.

Ben: What has a head, a tail, four legs, and sees equally well in all directions?
Len: You tell me.
Ben: A blind cow.

— ♦ —

Ben: What has webbed feet, fangs, and flies?
Len: I give up.
Ben: Count Quackula.

— ♦ —

Ben: What is the difference between a mailbox and a gorilla?
Len: Who knows?
Ben: If you don't know, I'll never let you mail my letters!

— ♦ —

Ben: What is bright, sits on a table, and wobbles a lot?
Len: You've got me.
Ben: Jellyvision.

— ♦ —

Ben: What is the difference between a sailor in jail and a blind man?
Len: My mind's a blank.
Ben: One can't see to go; the other can't go to sea.

Ben: What has two legs, two arms, and goes put, put, put, put, put?
Len: That's a mystery.
Ben: A very poor golfer.

— ◆ —

Ben: What is the laziest letter in the alphabet?
Len: I'm a blank.
Ben: The letter E because it is always in bed.

— ◆ —

Ben: What's a Hindu?
Len: I don't have the foggiest.
Ben: It lays eggs.

— ◆ —

Ben: What did Adam say to Eve on December 24?
Len: It's unknown to me.
Ben: It's Christmas Eve.

— ◆ —

Ben: What kind of work do lady mice do?
Len: I'm in the dark.
Ben: They do mousework.

— ◆ —

Ben: What's brown, quacks, and robs safes?
Len: Search me.
Ben: A safe quacker.

Ben: What is the safest way to talk to a hungry lion?
Len: You've got me guessing.
Ben: By long-distance telephone.

— ♦ —

Ben: What's green, bumpy, and pecks at trees?
Len: I pass.
Ben: Woody Wood Pickle.

— ♦ —

Ben: What's brown, crazy, and lives in South America?
Len: How should I know?
Ben: A Brazil nut.

What If?

Q: If the alphabet moves from A to Z, what moves from Z to A?
A: Zebra.

— ♦ —

Q: If they get honey from a bee, what do they get from a wasp?
A: Waspberry jam.

— ♦ —

Q: If 12 makes a dozen, how many make a million?
A: Very few.

Q: If an African lion fought an African tiger, which one do you think would win?
A: Neither one. There are no tigers in Africa.

— ◆ —

Q: If a papa bull eats five bales of hay, and a baby bull eats one bale of hay, how many bales of hay will a mama bull eat?
A: There is no such thing as a mama bull.

— ◆ —

Q: If they use pigskin for making shoes, what do they make out of banana skins?
A: Slippers.

— ◆ —

Q: If an apple a day keeps the doctor away, what does Limburger cheese do?
A: It keeps everyone away.

— ◆ —

Q: If 16 girls share a chocolate cake, what time is it?
A: A quarter to four.

— ◆ —

Q: If you had a splitting headache, what would be the best thing to take?
A: Glue-covered aspirin.

Q: If bees were to go on strike, what would be their reason?
A: Shorter flowers and more honey.

— ♦ —

Q: If you mixed together the white of an egg and a pound of gunpowder, what would you have?
A: A boom-meringue.

Lucy & Lacy

Lucy: What is gray, sits on buildings, and is very dangerous?
Lacy: I have no clue.
Lucy: A pigeon with a machine gun.

— ♦ —

Lucy: What do they call a lumberjack who fells trees and shouts too late?
Lacy: I have no idea.
Lucy: Tim.

— ♦ —

Lucy: What is orange, has stripes, and lives at the North Pole?
Lacy: I can't guess.
Lucy: A lost tiger.

Lucy: What has large antlers and frightens cats?
Lacy: I don't know.
Lucy: Mickey Moose.

— ◆ —

Lucy: What is the favorite year for a kangaroo?
Lacy: Beats me.
Lucy: Leap year.

— ◆ —

Lucy: What is the best way to file a knife?
Lacy: You tell me.
Lucy: Under the letter K.

— ◆ —

Lucy: What has one foot on each side and one foot in the middle?
Lacy: I give up.
Lucy: A yardstick.

— ◆ —

Lucy: What type of clothes do they put on a house?
Lacy: Who knows?
Lucy: Address.

— ◆ —

Lucy: What do they call a spy who dies his hair?
Lacy: My mind's a blank.
Lucy: James Blond.

Lucy: Who wears a blue suit, a cape, and loves vegetable soup?
Lacy: You've got me.
Lucy: Souperman.

— ◆ —

Lucy: What is the first word a baby computer says?
Lacy: That's a mystery.
Lucy: Da-ta.

— ◆ —

Lucy: What kind of music do computers play?
Lacy: I'm a blank.
Lucy: Disk-o.

— ◆ —

Lucy: What is as big as an elephant but doesn't weigh anything?
Lacy: I don't have the foggiest.
Lucy: The shadow of an elephant.

— ◆ —

Lucy: What do they call a prehistoric skunk?
Lacy: It's unknown to me.
Lucy: Ex-stinct.

— ◆ —

Lucy: What is green, has big eyes, and eats like a pig?
Lacy: Search me.
Lucy: Kermit the Hog.

Lucy: What do they call a dinosaur that goes around wrecking everything?

Lacy: I'm in the dark.

Lucy: Tyrannosaurus Wrecks.

— ◆ —

Lucy: What do they call a dinosaur that has mud between its toes?

Lacy: You've got me guessing.

Lucy: Brown-toe Saurus.

— ◆ —

Lucy: What did the boy magnet say to the girl magnet?

Lacy: I pass.

Lucy: I find you very attractive.

Teacher & Student

Teacher: If you add 79,312 and 46,920, then divide the answer by 39, and multiply by 78, what would you get?

Student: The wrong answer.

— ◆ —

Teacher: Why didn't you turn in your homework?

Student: I was going to, but on the way to school I saw a boy in a lake and I jumped in to rescue him and my homework drowned.

Teacher: Why did the germ cross the microscope?
Student: To get to the other slide.

— ♦ —

Teacher: Why were you late in getting to school?
Student: I overslept.
Teacher: You mean that you sleep at home, too?

— ♦ —

Teacher: What are you doing?
Student: I was looking at the clock to see when the period would end.
Teacher: Time will pass. Will you?

— ♦ —

Teacher: I would like you to spell Tennessee.
Student: Okay. One-a-see, two-a-see, three-a-see…

— ♦ —

Teacher: Are you good at English?
Student: Yes and no.
Teacher: What do you mean by that?
Student: Yes, I'm no good at English.

— ♦ —

Teacher: Where does satisfaction come from?
Student: A satisfactory.

Teacher: Why are you late for school?
Student: I dreamed that I was playing basketball, and the game went into overtime.

— ◆ —

Teacher: Will you please spell banana for me.
Student: I don't believe I can.
Teacher: Why not?
Student: Well, I know how to start but I don't know when to stop.

— ◆ —

Teacher: I hope I didn't see you copying the test from your friend.
Student: I hope you didn't, too.

— ◆ —

Teacher: If your father borrows thirty dollars from me, and pays me back at two dollars a month for seven months, how much will he owe me at that time?
Student: Thirty dollars.
Teacher: It doesn't seem like you know much about math.
Student: It doesn't seem like you know much about my father.

— ◆ —

Teacher: Why are you late for school this time?
Student: I sprained my ankle running to the bus.
Teacher: That's a lame excuse.

Teacher: Why does lightning never strike in the same place twice?

Student: After lightning hits something, it's not the same place anymore.

— ◆ —

Teacher: I tried to teach you everything I know.

Student: I know, and I'm still ignorant.

— ◆ —

Teacher: What is a wasp?

Student: An insect that stings for its supper.

— ◆ —

Teacher: Give me a sentence with the word "fascinate" in it.

Student: If I had a sweater with ten buttons and two of them fell off, I could then only fasten eight.

— ◆ —

Teacher: Give me a sentence starting with I.

Student: Okay. I is...

Teacher: No, no! You do not say "I is." You say "I am."

Student: Okay. I am the ninth letter of the alphabet.

Odds & Ends

Sign in window of the local dry cleaners: We'll clean for you...we'll press for you...we'll even dye for you.

He: Some girls think I'm handsome, and some girls think I'm ugly. What do you think?

She: I agree with both groups of girls. You're pretty ugly.

— ◆ —

Fred: My next-door neighbors keep banging on the walls at all hours of the night.

Frank: Doesn't that bother you? How can you sleep?

Fred: I get plenty of sleep but it interferes with my tuba practice.

— ◆ —

Mark: What do they call a contented cannibal?

Leroy: Someone who's fed up with people.

— ◆ —

Did you hear about the baby that was so ugly the mother didn't push the baby carriage; she pulled it.

— ◆ —

Doctor: My, but you look a little pale.

Patient: It doesn't surprise me. I nearly kicked the bucket.

— ◆ —

Paul: What do they usually do at a cannibal wedding?

Pete: They toast the happy couple.

Fred: My next-door neighbors keep banging on the walls at all hours of the night.

Frank: Doesn't that bother you? How can you sleep?

Fred: I get plenty of sleep but it interferes with my tuba practice.

Father: Why do you have a big black eye, son?
Robert: I dropped a baseball bat on a foot.
Father: That doesn't explain the black eye.
Robert: Well, you see, it wasn't my foot.

— ♦ —

Did you hear about the sword swallower who wanted to put something away for a rainy day, so he swallowed an umbrella?

— ♦ —

Bart: What do you get if you cross a skunk with a boomerang?
Art: I give up, what?
Bart: A terrible smell you can't get rid of.

— ♦ —

Customer: I would like to get a dress to match my eyes.
Salesclerk: I'm sorry, madam, but we don't have any bloodshot dresses.

— ♦ —

Luke: A very funny thing happened to my mother in Denver.
Duke: That's strange. I thought you were born in Dallas.

Brother: Oh, I've got a splinter in my finger.
Sister: You must have been scratching your head.

— ♦ —

Eddie: I think it is best if you eat french fries with your fingers.
Freddie: Actually, I prefer to eat fingers separately.

— ♦ —

He: I wonder how long someone can live without a brain?
She: How old are you?

Slim & Clem

Slim: What type of running means walking?
Clem: I have no clue.
Slim: Running out of gas.

— ♦ —

Slim: What did Tennessee?
Clem: You tell me.
Slim: The same thing Arkansas.

— ♦ —

Slim: Which nation in the world travels the fastest?
Clem: My mind's a blank.
Slim: The Russians.

Slim: What is yellow, long, and goes slam-slam-slam-slam?

Clem: Beats me.

Slim: A four-door banana.

— ◆ —

Slim: What has towns without houses, rivers and lakes without any water, and parks and forests without any trees?

Clem: I don't know.

Slim: A road map.

— ◆ —

Slim: What do they call a thief who steals only Honda cars?

Clem: I can't guess.

Slim: A Hounda-taker (undertaker).

— ◆ —

Slim: What is the favorite TV program of automobile manufacturers?

Clem: I have no idea.

Slim: Car Tunes.

— ◆ —

Slim: What is big, hairy, and flies at 1,200 miles per hour to France?

Clem: I give up.

Slim: King Kongcorde.

Slim: What do they call a dinosaur that is always in a hurry?

Clem: Who knows?

Slim: A Prontosaurus.

— ◆ —

Slim: Who was the famous Greek who they think invented baseball?

Clem: I'm in the dark.

Slim: Homer.

— ◆ —

Slim: What do you call someone who steals library books and never brings them back?

Clem: That's a mystery.

Slim: A bookkeeper.

— ◆ —

Slim: What is long, likes water, and whistles "Dixie" backwards?

Clem: I'm a blank.

Slim: General Robert E. Eel.

— ◆ —

Slim: What do you call it when you use someone else's telephone?

Clem: I don't have the foggiest.

Slim: Free speech.

Slim: What kind of clothing does your pet cat wear?
Clem: It's unknown to me.
Slim: A petticoat.

— ◆ —

Slim: Why do most cars cry?
Clem: You've got me.
Slim: Because they have windshield weepers.

— ◆ —

Slim: What do they call a camel without any humps?
Clem: You've got me guessing.
Slim: Humphrey.

— ◆ —

Slim: What goes gobble, gobble, bang?
Clem: I pass.
Slim: A turkey in a minefield.

— ◆ —

Slim: If a cat swallows a duck, what is it called?
Clem: How should I know?
Slim: A duck-filled fatty-puss.

— ◆ —

Slim: What has spots and is very untrustworthy?
Clem: I don't know.
Slim: A cheetah.

Slim: If you crossed a computer with an elephant, what do you think you would have?
Clem: Search me.
Slim: A very big know-it-all.

Who's There?

Knock, knock.
Who's there?
Razor.
Razor who?
Razor hands...this is a holdup.

— ◆ —

Knock, knock.
Who's there?
Quacker.
Quacker who?
Quacker 'nother knock-knock joke before I leave.

— ◆ —

Knock, knock.
Who's there?
Police.
Police who?
Police open the door, it's cold outside.

Knock, knock.
Who's there?
Avenue.
Avenue who?
Avenue heard the good news, I've got more knock-knock jokes.

— ◆ —

Knock, knock.
Who's there?
Lyndon.
Lyndon who?
Lyndon me an ear, and I'll tell you another knock-knock joke.

— ◆ —

Knock, knock.
Who's there?
Luke.
Luke who?
Luke who's there before you open the door.

— ◆ —

Knock, knock.
Who's there?
Justice.
Justice who?
Justice I thought. No one's home.

Knock, knock.
Who's there?
Miniature.
Miniature who?
Miniature open your mouth, you may put your foot in it.

— ♦ —

Knock, knock.
Who's there?
Kent.
Kent who?
Kent you just wait until I tell you another knock-knock joke?

— ♦ —

Knock, knock.
Who's there?
Iguana.
Iguana who?
Iguana hold your hand . . .

— ♦ —

Knock, knock.
Who's there?
Izzy.
Izzy who?
Izzy come, Izzy go.

Knock, knock.
Who's there?
Hair.
Hair who?
Hair today, gone tomorrow.

— ◆ —

Knock, knock.
Who's there?
Freddie.
Freddie who?
Freddie or not... here I come!

— ◆ —

Knock, knock.
Who's there?
Heaven.
Heaven who?
Heaven seen you for a long, long time.

— ◆ —

Knock, knock.
Who's there?
Franz.
Franz who?
Franz... Romans... countrymen... lend me
your ears.

Knock, knock.
Who's there?
Hominy.
Hominy who?
Hominy times do I have to knock at your door?

— ♦ —

Knock, knock.
Who's there?
Hiram.
Hiram who?
Hiram fine, how are you?

— ♦ —

Knock, knock.
Who's there?
Gladys.
Gladys who?
Gladys see you.

— ♦ —

Knock, knock.
Who's there?
Grammar.
Grammar who?
Grammar crackers. Pretty crummy, huh?

Knock, knock.
Who's there?
Fresno.
Fresno who?
Rudolf the Fresno reindeer.

Hoarse Laughs

He: May I hold your hand?
She: It isn't very heavy. I think I can carry it myself.

— ◆ —

"Look at that girl over there. She's wearing boy's jeans, a boy's shirt, and her haircut looks like a boy's. It's hard to tell if she is a boy or a girl."
"She's a girl."
"How can you tell?"
"Easy. She happens to be my daughter."
"Oh, excuse me. I didn't know you were her father."
"I'm not. I'm her mother."

— ◆ —

It is true that an elephant never forgets. But then, what does he have to remember?

— ◆ —

Grandson: Grandad, is it fun being 97?
Grandad: It certainly is. If I wasn't 97, I'd be dead.

Someone has said that teenagers brighten the home. This is because they never turn off the lights.

— ♦ —

Did you hear about the drunk elephant? He had real problems. He went around seeing pink people.

— ♦ —

Jill: A donkey wanted to eat some green grass, but the grass was on the other side of a river. There was no bridge. No boat. And the donkey couldn't swim. How did he get across?
Bill: I give up.
Jill: So did the donkey.

— ♦ —

Betty: I hear you advertised for a husband in a magazine. Did you have any luck?
Karla: Yes, I had 72 answers, and they all said the same thing.
Betty: What was that?
Karla: You can have mine!

— ♦ —

David: You're such a stupid numskull.
Father: David, I told you before not to talk to your sister that way. Now, say you're sorry.
David: I'm sorry you're such a stupid numskull.

Father: I told you not to walk on top of that fence. You could get hurt.

Willie: Oh, I'll be all right. I'm good at this.

Father: Well, if you fall and break both your legs, don't come running to me.

— ♦ —

Mick: I saw silly Sam salting salmon. How many S's are in that?

Rick: I give up.

Mick: There aren't any S's in that!

— ♦ —

Bart: If a purple house has purple bricks, an orange house has orange bricks, a pink house has pink bricks, and a white house has white bricks, what color bricks does a green house have?

Art: I give up.

Bart: A greenhouse doesn't have bricks. It's made of glass.

— ♦ —

Pam: Two boys were born on the same day and to the same parents. They looked alike and behaved alike, but they were not twins. How could this be?

Melba: I don't know.

Pam: Because they were two brothers of a set of triplets!

Clyde: Did you hear about the crazy person who went around saying no all the time?

Leroy: No.

Clyde: I think I've found him.

— ◆ —

Larry: Let's have a race to see who can say the alphabet first.

Gary: Okay. I'm ready.

Larry: The alphabet.

— ◆ —

Son: Daddy, I don't like this cheese with holes.

Father: Just eat the cheese and leave the holes on the side of your plate.

— ◆ —

Wife: Thank heavens you're here, Doctor. My husband says he's so sick that he wants to die.

Doctor: You did the right thing in sending for me.

Melba & Pam

Melba: What has two legs, a trunk, and is very green?

Pam: A seasick tourist.

Melba: What is the most dangerous vegetable to have in a boat?

Pam: A leek.

— ◆ —

Melba: What is the best day to get a suntan at the beach?

Pam: On Sunday.

— ◆ —

Melba: What goes around a school but does not move?

Pam: A fence.

— ◆ —

Melba: What do they call the meanest apple?

Pam: A crab apple.

— ◆ —

Melba: What insect gets the best grades in English class?

Pam: The spelling bee.

— ◆ —

Melba: What doesn't get any wetter no matter how hard it rains?

Pam: A lake.

Melba: What time is spelled forward and backward yet remains the same?
Pam: Noon.

— ♦ —

Melba: What do they call the animal that is a cross between an insect and a rabbit?
Pam: Bugs Bunny.

— ♦ —

Melba: What does the baby elephant do when the daddy elephant is about to sneeze?
Pam: He gets out of the way fast.

— ♦ —

Melba: What kind of party does Frosty the Snowman go to?
Pam: The snowball.

— ♦ —

Melba: What is the name of the famous author who wrote about french fries?
Pam: Edgar Allan Poe-tato.

— ♦ —

Melba: There is a boy named "Fraidy Cat." What is his favorite food?
Pam: Chicken.

Melba: What do boxers like to drink the best?
Pam: Punch.

— ◆ —

Melba: If a ghost had a ghost rooster, what would it say?
Pam: Cock-a-doodle-boo.

— ◆ —

Melba: What is the best way to take the temperature of a giraffe?
Pam: With a verrrrrry long thermometer.

— ◆ —

Melba: What time is it when you are being chased by six angry tigers?
Pam: Six after one.

— ◆ —

Melba: If a ghost were to make a mistake, what would you call it?
Pam: A boo-boo.

— ◆ —

Melba: What would you call a skeleton that wouldn't do any yard work?
Pam: Lazy bones.

Tie Your Tongue in a Knot
Say the following phrases three times...real fast.

Big brass bombers bomb blue buildings.

— ◆ —

Sally safely sells seven shapely socks.

— ◆ —

Peggy Paddock peddles Ping-Pong paddles.

— ◆ —

Three free figs float freely.

— ◆ —

Frances fries fine fish for Frank's father's fish fry.

— ◆ —

Simeon's slippery ship is shipshape, sir.

— ◆ —

Fred Farley found a fish-and-chip shop with fine fish-sauce.

— ◆ —

Big beefy Billy Baker bakes black bread badly.

Sixty-six sick sheep slept silently in the Sheik's sheep shop.

— ◆ —

Mixed biscuits boxed badly are mixed by the biscuit mixer.

— ◆ —

She said Suzie sheared six shabby sheep slowly.

— ◆ —

The back black brake block box broke badly.

— ◆ —

Sixty sleepy sheep shun sunshine shearing.

— ◆ —

Scented cinnamon chrysanthemums set on aluminum linoleum.

— ◆ —

The small shiny silver sign signifies sharks swimming.

— ◆ —

Susan shocked silly Sally with shocking shoes and socks.

Mixed biscuits boxed badly are mixed by the biscuit mixer.

Joe & Moe

Joe: What is the largest mouse in the world?
Moe: I have no clue.
Joe: Hippopota-mouse.

— ◆ —

Joe: What is brown and travels underground at over a hundred miles per hour?
Moe: I don't know.
Joe: A gopher on a motorcycle.

— ◆ —

Joe: What does the Lone Ranger say when he drops off his garbage?
Moe: Beats me.
Joe: To-de-dump, to-de-dump, to-de-dump-dump-dump...

— ◆ —

Joe: What illness is common in China?
Moe: You tell me.
Joe: Kung Flu.

— ◆ —

Joe: What is the most silent tongue?
Moe: My mind is a blank.
Joe. The tongue in your shoe.

Joe: What do you get when you dial (209) 557-3796-643-2239 Extension # 7956?

Moe: I can't guess.

Joe: A blister on your finger.

— ♦ —

Joe: What is the name for people who walk around with an encyclopedia in their back pocket?

Moe: I have no idea.

Joe: Smarty pants.

— ♦ —

Joe: What did the stamp say to the envelope?

Moe: I give up.

Joe: Stick with me buddy, and we will go places together.

— ♦ —

Joe: What is the name of the invention that enables you to see through the thickest walls?

Moe: Who knows?

Joe: A window.

— ♦ —

Joe: What has a mouth and does not speak, and a bed and does not sleep?

Moe: You've got me.

Joe: A river.

Joe: After trees are chopped down, what do you do?

Moe: That's a mystery.

Joe: Simple. Chop them up.

— ◆ —

Joe: What occurs once in every minute, twice in every moment, but not once in a thousand years?

Moe: I'm a blank.

Joe: The letter M.

— ◆ —

Joe: What is the hardest thing about learning to ice-skate?

Moe: I don't have the foggiest.

Joe: The ice.

— ◆ —

Joe: What gets wetter as it dries?

Moe: It's unknown to me.

Joe: A paper towel.

— ◆ —

Joe: What wears a coat all winter and pants in the summer?

Moe: I'm in the dark.

Joe: A dog.

Joe: If ghosts had a favorite song, what would it be?

Moe: Search me.

Joe: A haunting melody.

— ♦ —

Joe: What do you call a very friendly and handsome monster?

Moe: I pass.

Joe: A failure.

Lisa & Christy

Lisa: How does a farmer count his cows?

Christy: I have no clue.

Lisa: On a cowculator.

— ♦ —

Lisa: What is the best way to avoid being driven crazy?

Christy: I don't know.

Lisa: Walk.

— ♦ —

Lisa: What do you use to mend a broken heart?

Christy: Beats me.

Lisa: Ticker tape.

Lisa: How much does a psychiatrist charge a hippopotamus?

Christy: I can't guess.

Lisa: Fifty dollars for the hour and $700 for the couch.

— ♦ —

Lisa: How does an Indian fix a tepee that has holes in it?

Christy: I have no idea.

Lisa: Apache here, Apache there.

— ♦ —

Lisa: What did the man say when he got the bill from the electric company?

Christy: You tell me.

Lisa: I'm shocked.

— ♦ —

Lisa: What do you say to an astronomer about his business?

Christy: I give up.

Lisa: Is your business looking up?

— ♦ —

Lisa: How do you make a kangaroo stew?

Christy: That's a mystery.

Lisa: Keep him waiting for three hours.

Lisa: How do vegetables travel from the field to the grocery store?

Christy: Who knows?

Lisa: They take a taxi cabbage.

— ♦ —

Lisa: What did the tailor say when he was asked how his business was?

Christy: You've got me.

Lisa: Sew-sew.

— ♦ —

Lisa: What is the best way to keep a rhinoceros from charging?

Christy: My mind's a blank.

Lisa: Take away his MasterCard.

— ♦ —

Lisa: If you had a sore throat and fleas at the same time, how would you feel?

Christy: I don't have the foggiest.

Lisa: Hoarse and buggy.

— ♦ —

Lisa: What is the first thing you say to a pier?

Christy: It's unknown to me.

Lisa: What's up, Dock!

Lisa: What swimming stroke do babies use?
Christy: I'm in the dark.
Lisa: The crawl.

— ◆ —

Lisa: What is the best way to say good-bye to the ocean?
Christy: Search me.
Lisa: Wave.

— ◆ —

Lisa: When the chicken forgot its lines in the school play, what did Barbie the dramatics teacher do to help?
Christy: You've got me guessing.
Lisa: Barbie cued the chicken.

— ◆ —

Lisa: When someone asked the author how his business was doing, what did he say?
Christy: I pass.
Lisa: It's all write.

— ◆ —

Lisa: How do you know that dodo birds are smarter than chickens?
Christy: I have no clue.
Lisa: Have you ever heard of Kentucky Fried Dodo Bird?

Lisa: How do you get eggs from a golden eagle?
Christy: How should I know?
Lisa: You walk up to the golden eagle and say, "This is a stickup!"

— ♦ —

Lisa: What is the fastest way to make a mothball?
Christy: I don't know.
Lisa: Hit it in the mouth.

— ♦ —

Lisa: How do they make a Venetian blind?
Christy: Beats me.
Lisa: Stick a finger in his eye.

— ♦ —

Lisa: How do you make a Swiss roll?
Christy: I can't guess.
Lisa: Take him to the top of one of the mountains in the Swiss Alps and push him off.

— ♦ —

Lisa: Is it true that Jon-Mark swam a hundred meters in two seconds?
Christy: Yes, it is. He went over a waterfall.

Knee Slappers

My boyfriend is very polite. He always takes off his shoes before he puts his feet on the table.

Billy: You're a natural musician.
Willie: What do you mean by that?
Billy: Your tongue is sharp and your head is flat.

— ◆ —

I don't want to say that the food in our school cafeteria is bad, but you get a prescription with every meal.

— ◆ —

Bart: You know, I've had this tune running through my head all day. I can't seem to stop it.
Art: That's because there is nothing there to get in the way of it.

— ◆ —

Boy: Did you miss me while I was away?
Girl: Were you away?

— ◆ —

First Mother: I finally got my son to stop biting his nails.
Second Mother: How did you do that?
First Mother: I bought him some shoes.

— ◆ —

Melenda: I think I just swallowed a bug.
Russell: You'd better take something for it.
Melenda: No. I think I'll just let it starve.

Jack: What was the name of the man who wrote My Terrible Life of Crime?

Linda: I believe that was Robin Banks.

— ♦ —

Noll: Mom, I just knocked over the ladder that was leaning against the tree outside.

Mother: Well, I think you had better tell your father.

Noll: He already knows about it. He was on the top of the ladder.

— ♦ —

Carla: This restaurant makes the best UFO meals.

Marla: What in the world is a UFO meal?

Carla: Unidentified Frying Objects.

— ♦ —

Ned: Why did the turkey cross the road?

Ted: I don't know... why?

Ned: To get his old-age pension. Get it?

Ted: No.

Ned: Neither did the turkey.

— ♦ —

Husband: What did you think of the picture they took of me?

Wife: I think that it makes you look five years older.

Husband: Oh, well, that will save me from having one taken five years from now.

Husband: Who is ringing the doorbell?
Wife: It is someone who is selling beehives.
Husband: Tell him to buzz off.

— ♦ —

Bob: I value your opinion. What do you think of the latest joke book that I have written?
Ken: Frankly, it's worthless.
Bob: I know, but I'd like to hear your opinion just the same.

— ♦ —

Christy: I heard that someone in Russia owns a talking cow. Do you know who it is?
Lisa: I think it is Ma's cow.

Gary & Larry

Gary: What is the difference between a light sleeper and a butcher?
Larry: I have no clue.
Gary: One weighs a steak and the other stays awake.

— ♦ —

Gary: What is the best thing to do for a very sick wasp?
Larry: I don't know.
Gary: Take it to the waspital.

Gary: What is the strangest thing about carpets?
Larry: Beats me.
Gary: They're bought by the yard and worn by the foot.

— ◆ —

Gary: What is the difference between a circus owner who yells and a barber who lived in ancient Rome?
Larry: I can't guess.
Gary: One is a shaving Roman and the other is a raving showman.

— ◆ —

Gary: What would you say to a man who came to the door with a tuba?
Larry: I have no idea.
Gary: I'd tell him to blow.

— ◆ —

Gary: What is the reason that people laugh up their sleeves?
Larry: You tell me.
Gary: Because that is where their funnybone is.

— ◆ —

Gary: What would happen if pigs had wings and could fly?
Larry: I give up.
Gary: Bacon would go up.

Gary: What type of airplane does the Pope like to fly in?

Larry: Who knows?

Gary: A holy-copter.

— ◆ —

Gary: What is doughy, covered with tomato paste, and is 50 yards high?

Larry: You've got me.

Gary: The Leaning Tower of Pizza.

— ◆ —

Gary: What would happen if you tickled the ivories?

Larry: My mind is a blank.

Gary: It would make the piano laugh.

— ◆ —

Gary: What is the difference between a school-teacher and a railway engineer?

Larry: That's a mystery.

Gary: One minds the train and the other trains the mind.

— ◆ —

Gary: What should you do if your nose goes on strike?

Larry: My mind is a blank.

Gary: Pick-it.

Gary: What is the best thing to do with a blue cow?
Larry: I don't have the foggiest.
Gary: Cheer her up.

— ◆ —

Gary: What weighs many tons, is 900 feet tall, and attracts bees?
Larry: It's unknown to me.
Gary: The Eiffel Flower.

— ◆ —

Gary: What has long hair, weighs 2,000 pounds, and carries a flower?
Larry: I'm in the dark.
Gary: A hippie-potamus.

— ◆ —

Gary: What time of day would it be if you had a toothache?
Larry: Search me.
Gary: Tooth-hurty.

— ◆ —

Gary: What is blue, big, and goes around pouting all day?
Larry: You've got me guessing.
Gary: The Incredible Sulk.

Gary: What would you call a man with a shovel in his head?

Larry: I pass.

Gary: Doug.

— ♦ —

Gary: What do you get if you cross a hippopotamus with a kangaroo?

Larry: How should I know?

Gary: Great big holes all over Australia.

Where, Oh Where

Q: Where do Batman and Robin go when they get dirty?

A: Straight to the bat-tub.

— ♦ —

Q: Where do you find out the most information about chickens?

A: In the Hen-cyclopedia.

— ♦ —

Q: Where do you take a squid that is very sick?

A: To the doc-topus.

— ♦ —

Q: Where do calves eat?

A: In the calf-eteria.

Q: Where does Frosty the Snowman keep all of his money?
A: In a snowbank.

— ♦ —

Q: Where does Superman get the food he needs to make him strong?
A: At the supermarket.

— ♦ —

Q: Where do chickens dance?
A: At the fowl ball.

— ♦ —

Q: Where do very strange people go for a vacation?
A: To Lake Erie.

— ♦ —

Q: Where do fish like to go for a vacation?
A: Finland.

— ♦ —

Q: Where is the best place to take a sick duck?
A: To the duck-tor.

— ♦ —

Q: Where do old Volkswagon cars end up?
A: In the Old Volks Home.

Q: Where do King Arthur's knights go to study?
A: Knight school.

— ◆ —

Q: Where does the sandman like to keep his sleeping sand?
A: In his knapsack.

— ◆ —

Q: Where do squirrels go when they are crazy?
A: To the nut house.

— ◆ —

Q: Where do you take a sick ocean liner?
A: To the dock.

— ◆ —

Q: Where can you always find success, health, wealth, and happiness?
A: In the dictionary.

— ◆ —

Q: Where were chickens first fried?
A: In Greece.

— ◆ —

Q: Where do golfers go to dance?
A: To the golf ball.

Q: Where can you always find diamonds if you look for them?
A: In a deck of cards.

— ◆ —

Q: Where do cows love to go for their vacation?
A: Moo York.

— ◆ —

Q: Where is the best place to find a prehistoric cow?
A: In the moo-seum.

Luke & Duke

Luke: What lies on the ground 100 feet in the air?
Duke: I have no idea.
Luke: A centipede on its back.

— ◆ —

Luke: What sea creature will not do anything without a good reason.
Duke: I don't know.
Luke: A porpoise (purpose).

— ◆ —

Luke: What do you call a cow without any legs?
Duke: Beats me.
Luke: Ground beef.

Luke: What is the name of the laziest mountain in all the world?
Duke: I can't guess.
Luke: Mount Everest.

— ◆ —

Luke: What kind of umbrella does the president of Canada carry on a rainy day?
Duke: I have no idea.
Luke: A wet one.

— ◆ —

Luke: What is the distance between the ears of a very, very stupid person?
Duke: You tell me.
Luke: Next to nothing.

— ◆ —

Luke: What do they call someone who thinks he can fly by flapping his arms?
Duke: It's unknown to me.
Luke: Plane crazy.

— ◆ —

Luke: What is the fastest way to make a banana split?
Duke: Who knows?
Luke: Cut it in half.

Luke: What do they call someone who thinks he can fly by flapping his arms?

Duke: It's unknown to me.

Luke: Plane crazy.

Luke: What is purple and over 5,000 miles long?
Duke: My mind is a blank.
Luke: The Grape Wall of China.

— ◆ —

Luke: What is the best way to fix the broken tooth of a gorilla?
Duke: You've got me guessing.
Luke: With a monkey wrench.

— ◆ —

Luke: What is more invisible than the invisible man?
Duke: I give up.
Luke: The shadow of the invisible man.

— ◆ —

Luke: What is the best thing to put angel food cake into?
Duke: I'm in the dark.
Luke: Your teeth.

— ◆ —

Luke: What would be the best thing to do if you found you had water on the knee, water on the elbow, and water on the brain?
Duke: Search me.
Luke: Turn off the shower.

Luke: What do you give a seasick hippopotamus?
Duke: How should I know?
Luke: Plenty of room.

— ♦ —

Luke: How do you keep milk from turning sour?
Duke: I'm a blank.
Luke: Keep it in the cow.

— ♦ —

Luke: What is green and goes up and down?
Duke: I don't have the foggiest.
Luke: A pickle in an elevator.

— ♦ —

Luke: What did the farmer do when he found that 300 hares escaped from his rabbit farm?
Duke: I pass.
Luke: He combed the area.

Open the Door

Knock, knock.
Who's there?
Thumping.
Thumping who?
Thumping green and slimy is crawling on your shoulder.

Knock, knock.
Who's there?
Romeo.
Romeo who?
Romeo-cross the lake in a canoe.

— ♦ —

Knock, knock.
Who's there?
Jethro.
Jethro who?
Jethro the canoe and stop talking.

— ♦ —

Knock, knock.
Who's there?
Rhoda.
Rhoda who?
Rhoda horse back after crossing the lake.

— ♦ —

Knock, knock.
Who's there?
Utah Nevada.
Utah Nevada who?
Utah Nevada guess where you went for a vacation.

Knock, knock.
Who's there?
Doughnut.
Doughnut who?
Doughnut close the door, my foot is in it.

— ◆ —

Knock, knock.
Who's there?
Ferdie.
Ferdie who?
Ferdie last time, will you please open the door? My foot is still in it.

— ◆ —

Knock, knock.
Who's there?
Handover.
Handover who?
Handover your money, this is a stickup.

— ◆ —

Knock, knock.
Who's there?
Dick.
Dick who?
Dick 'em up! I told you this was a holdup.

Knock, knock.
Who's there?
Egypt.
Egypt who?
Egypt me, and I want my mummy back.

— ◆ —

Knock, knock.
Who's there?
Zeke.
Zeke who?
Zeke and ye shall find, knock and the door will be opened.

— ◆ —

Knock, knock.
Who's there?
Zippy.
Zippy who?
Zippy de do da ... Zippy de da ... my, oh my, what a wonderful day.

— ◆ —

Knock, knock.
Who's there?
Zippy.
Zippy who?
Mrs. Zippy. Can you spell that without any I's?

Knock, knock.
Who's there?
Yachts.
Yachts who?
Yachts up, Doc?

— ◆ —

Knock, knock.
Who's there?
Yah.
Yah who?
Ride 'em, cowboy!

— ◆ —

Knock, knock.
Who's there?
Whittle.
Whittle who?
Whittle Orphan Annie.

— ◆ —

Knock, knock.
Who's there?
Tibet.
Tibet who?
Early Tibet and early to rise, makes a man healthy, wealthy, and wise.

Knock, knock.
Who's there?
Utica.
Utica who?
Utica high road, and I'll take the low road.

— ♦ —

Knock, knock.
Who's there?
Toyota.
Toyota who?
Toyota be a law against knock-knock jokes.

— ♦ —

Knock, knock.
Who's there?
Turnip.
Turnip who?
Turnip the heat. It's cold in the house.

— ♦ —

Knock, knock.
Who's there?
Tibet.
Tibet who?
Tibet you can't guess who's knocking at the door.

Knock, knock.
Who's there?
Sybil.
Sybil who?
Sybil Simon met a pieman.

— ◆ —

Knock, knock.
Who's there?
Sherwood.
Sherwood who?
Sherwood be good if someone did away with knock-knock jokes.

— ◆ —

Knock, knock.
Who's there?
Sherwood.
Sherwood who?
Sherwood be nice if you would let me in.

— ◆ —

Knock, knock.
Who's there?
Sheila.
Sheila who?
Sheila be coming round the mountain when she comes...

Knock, knock.
Who's there?
Rufus.
Rufus who?
Rufus leaking and I'm getting wet.

— ◆ —

Knock, knock.
Who's there?
Rocky.
Rocky who?
Rocky bye baby, in the tree top...

Side Splitters

Lisa: What is one and one?
Christy: Two.
Lisa: What is four minus two?
Christy: Two.
Lisa: Who wrote Tom Sawyer?
Christy: Twain.
Lisa: Now say all the answers together.
Christy: Two, two, Twain.
Lisa: Have a nice trip.

— ◆ —

Bart: What do you get if you cross a silkworm with a hen?
Art: A chicken that lays eggs with panty hose inside.

Judge: Mr. Punster, you drove through a red light. The fine will be $50. The next time, you will go to jail. Do you understand?

Driver: Yes, sir, your honor. Just like a weather report. Fine today, cooler tomorrow.

— ♦ —

Did you hear about the porcupine who bumped into a cactus? "Is that you sweetheart?" He asked tenderly.

— ♦ —

Susan: What do you get when you cross a cow with a tortoise?

Peggy: A turtleneck jersey.

— ♦ —

Did you hear about the generation crisis in reverse? A teenager drove his car into the garage and ran over his father's bicycle.

— ♦ —

Tomcat: I love you so much. I would even die for you.

Pussycat: Yes, but how many times?

— ♦ —

Rob: What is the best way to prevent disease caused by biting insects?

P.K.: Don't bite any.

Patient: Doctor, what is the best thing to do when your ear rings?

Doctor: Answer it.

— ◆ —

Paul: Did Adam and Eve ever have a date?

Jeff: No, I think they only had an apple.

— ◆ —

Nit: I can lift an elephant with one hand.

Wit: That's impossible. I don't believe it.

Nit: Okay, show me an elephant with one hand and I'll prove it.

— ◆ —

Pam: Modeen went swimming and saw a shark.

Melba: Was she afraid?

Pam: No, she wasn't.

Melba: Why not?

Pam: Because it was a man-eating shark.

— ◆ —

Ian: Who cut your hair that way?

P.K.: My barber.

Ian: What did he use?

P.K.: He used a sword.

Ian: What is his name?

P.K.: Conan the barbar, Ian.

Ken: What is the name of the science-fiction hero who plays hockey?

Bob: Puck Rogers.

— ♦ —

Programmer: I am afraid that your computer is dead.

Operator: What did it die of?

Programmer: A terminal illness.

— ♦ —

Did you hear about the lady who had a home computer? When she wasn't around, her young son, Hans, would play with the keys. He would always play with the keys after he had eaten something. He would get peanut butter and jelly and all kinds of sticky things on the keys.

After awhile, the computer could stand the mess no longer. One day when the lady turned on the computer the following message was on the screen: *I won't do any work for you until you take your dirty Hans off me!*

— ♦ —

Clark: Don't you think I have savoir faire?

Clara: I don't think you even have carfare.

— ♦ —

Lisa: Have you ever seen a porpoise cry?

Christy: No, but I've seen whales blubber.

George: What's the difference between a pickle and a snoo?

Harry: What's a snoo?

George: Not much. What's snoo with you?

Bertie & Gertie

Bertie: Why is a hot dog better than a stray dog?

Gertie: I have no clue.

Bertie: Because it doesn't bite the hand that feeds it. Instead it feeds the one that bites it.

— ◆ —

Bertie: What floats when it's off and flies when it's on?

Gertie: I don't know.

Bertie: A feather.

— ◆ —

Bertie: When a pig writes a letter, what does it use?

Gertie: Beats me.

Bertie: Pen and oink.

— ◆ —

Bertie: What do you get if you cross a goose and a rhinoceros?

Gertie: I can't guess.

Bertie: An animal that honks before it runs over you.

Bertie: What kind of socks do baseball players like to wear?
Gertie: I have no idea.
Bertie: Socks with runs in them.

— ♦ —

Bertie: What is the quietest sport that is played?
Gertie: You tell me.
Bertie: Bowling, because you can hear a pin drop.

— ♦ —

Bertie: What goes up and down but does not move?
Gertie: I'm in the dark.
Bertie: A ladder.

— ♦ —

Bertie: What is the biggest building in town?
Gertie: You've got me.
Bertie: The library. It has the most stories.

— ♦ —

Bertie: Why did your jacket catch on fire?
Gertie: My mind is a blank.
Bertie: It was a blazer.

— ♦ —

Bertie: Who are most of the fish in the ocean afraid of?
Gertie: That's a mystery.
Bertie: Jack the Kipper.

Bertie: What do they call a freight train loaded with bubble gum?

Gertie: I'm a blank.

Bertie: A chew-chew train.

— ♦ —

Bertie: What has two eyes like a kangaroo, two legs like a kangaroo, and looks like a kangaroo, but is not a kangaroo?

Gertie: I don't have the foggiest.

Bertie: A picture of a kangaroo.

— ♦ —

Bertie: What is a female deer after it is seven months old?

Gertie: It's unknown to me.

Bertie: Eight months old.

— ♦ —

Bertie: If you take your hair dryer and blow it down a rabbit hole, what happens?

Gertie: Who knows?

Bertie: You get hot, cross bunnies.

— ♦ —

Bertie: What do they call the strongest bird in the world?

Gertie: Search me.

Bertie: A crane.

Here's a Mouthful

Say the following phrases three times ... real fast.

Seven shameful sharks slashed satin sheets.

— ◆ —

Just Judge Jerry Jennings judges justly.

— ◆ —

Salty Sam shoots Sally's snapshot swiftly.

— ◆ —

Silly sharpshooters should safely shoot slowly.

— ◆ —

The sharp shark shop sells short silk shorts.

— ◆ —

Selfish Sheriff Sam Short should share some shellfish.

— ◆ —

Three sly shy thrushes.

— ◆ —

Free thugs set three thugs free.

Should selfish Sheriff Sam Short sup soup at cheap chop suey shops?

— ♦ —

The sailing suave sharpshooting sailors are shipshape, sir.

— ♦ —

Surely the soft summer sun shall shine soon.

— ♦ —

He says she says she shall sew satin sheets shut.

— ♦ —

Sulky Sascha slightly sews slashed sheets slowly.

— ♦ —

Should she shun such silly subjects?

Sidney & Leroy

Sidney: What do you call a person who doesn't have all of his toes on one foot?

Leroy: Beats me.

Sidney: Normal. Toes are supposed to be on both feet.

Sidney: What do they call a criminal who doesn't take a bath?
Leroy: I have no clue.
Sidney: A dirty crook.

— ◆ —

Sidney: How do you cure dandruff?
Leroy: I don't know.
Sidney: Go bald.

— ◆ —

Sidney: Why did the timid doctor tiptoe past the medicine cabinet?
Leroy: I can't guess.
Sidney: He didn't want to wake up the sleeping pills.

— ◆ —

Sidney: What is the best cure for acid indigestion?
Leroy: I have no idea.
Sidney: Stop drinking acid.

— ◆ —

Sidney: If you cross a Boy Scout with a kangaroo, what do you get?
Leroy: Who knows?
Sidney: A kangaroo that helps old ladies hop across the street.

Sidney: What is the best water for your health?
Leroy: You tell me.
Sidney: Well water.

— ◆ —

Sidney: What would be worse than a turtle with claustrophobia?
Leroy: I give up.
Sidney: An elephant with hay fever.

— ◆ —

Sidney: What is the cruelest type of person to have around babies?
Leroy: You've got me.
Sidney: A baby sitter.

— ◆ —

Sidney: When the man stepped on a candy bar, what did he say?
Leroy: I don't have the foggiest.
Sidney: I've set foot on Mars.

— ◆ —

Sidney: What happens to the little boy who misses the school bus?
Leroy: It's unknown to me.
Sidney: He catches it when he gets home.

Sidney: What is the best water for your health?
Leroy: You tell me.
Sidney: Well water.

Sidney: What do people in Tibet do when it rains?
Leroy: My mind's a blank.
Sidney: They let it rain.

— ◆ —

Sidney: What is gray, has sharp teeth, and holds up socks?
Leroy: I'm in the dark.
Sidney: An Alligarter.

— ◆ —

Sidney: When a dog graduates from obedience school what does he get?
Leroy: Search me.
Sidney: A pet-degree.

— ◆ —

Sidney: What is the major cause of baldness?
Leroy: You've got me guessing.
Sidney: Lack of hair.

— ◆ —

Sidney: What two words have the most letters in them?
Leroy: I pass.
Sidney: Post Office.

School Daze

Teacher: Laura, please tell me where your right foot was located when you fell down and got hurt.

Student: My right foot was located at the end of my right leg.

— ♦ —

Teacher: Now Willard, before we go out for recess, I want you to answer some questions. Remember, all of your responses must be oral. Do you understand?

Student: Oral.

Teacher: How many letters are there in the alphabet?

Student: Oral.

— ♦ —

Teacher: Gerald, what can you tell me about the Dead Sea?

Student: Gee whiz, I didn't even know it was sick!

— ♦ —

Teacher: Mary, how much is half of 8?

Student: Up and down or across?

Teacher: What do you mean?

Student: Up and down it's 3, and across it is 0.

Teacher: Alfred   hat is the highest form of animal life?
Student: The giraffe.

— ◆ —

Teacher: Martin, where is the English Channel located?
Student: I have no idea. My television set doesn't pick it up.

— ◆ —

Teacher: Roy, what is the name of the school you have to drop out of in order to graduate?
Student: Parachute school.

— ◆ —

Teacher: Roger, how is it possible for one person like yourself to make so many mistakes in one day?
Student: I get up early.

— ◆ —

Teacher: Dale, can you tell me why there is a Mother's Day and a Father's Day, but no Son's Day?
Student: Because there is a Sunday in every week.

— ◆ —

Teacher: Evans, how do you make Mexican chili?
Student: Take him to the North Pole.

Teacher: Ken, here is a hard question. Name an animal that lives in Lapland.

Student: A reindeer.

Teacher: That's great. Now name another.

Student: Another reindeer.

— ◆ —

Teacher: Rich, the class has been a little slow in answering questions. The next question I want you to answer at once. What month comes after September?

Student: At once.

— ◆ —

I don't want to say that the food in our cafeteria is bad, but the flies go there to commit suicide.

— ◆ —

Did you hear about the mother who sent an excuse note to school? It read, "Please excuse my son's tardiness. I forgot to wake him up, and I did not find him till I started making the bed."

Belly Laughs

First Prisoner: What are you in for?

Second Prisoner: I was driving my car too slow.

First Prisoner: Too slow! Don't you mean driving too fast?

Second Prisoner: No, too slow. The police caught me after I robbed the store.

Jeff: How was your first day on the job as a chimney cleaner?

Don: Well, it soots me.

— ◆ —

Jeff: Who went into the lions' den and came out alive?

Noll: Daniel.

Jeff: That's great. You're right. Who went into the tigers' den and came out alive?

Noll: I don't know.

Jeff: The tiger!

— ◆ —

A man went into a pet store to buy a parrot. He noticed that one of the parrots had a red ribbon tied to one foot and a blue ribbon tied to the other foot.

Customer: Why does that parrot have ribbons tied to each of its feet?

Salesclerk: That is a very special parrot. He was trained to talk by pulling one of the ribbons. If you pull the red ribbon, the parrot will recite Psalm 23 from the Bible. If you pull the blue ribbon, the parrot will recite the Gettysburg Address by Abraham Lincoln.

Customer: What happens if you pull both ribbons at the same time?

At this point the parrot screeched, "I will fall off my perch, stupid!"

Daughter: Dad, there is a man at the door collecting for the new swimming pool in the park.

Father: Okay. Give him a bucket of water.

— ♦ —

A big-mouthed Texan was being shown the sights of London by a taxi driver.

Texan: What's that building?

Taxi Driver: Buckingham Place. The Queen lives there.

Texan: Back in Texas, we could put up a building like that in a month.

Taxi Driver: Oh, really?

Texan: What is that building?

Taxi Driver: That is the Tower of London.

Texan: Humph! Back in Texas, we could put up a building like that in two weeks.

Taxi Driver: Oh, really?

Texan: By the way, isn't that Westminster Abbey on the corner?

Taxi Driver: I am afraid I don't know, governor. The building wasn't there yesterday.

— ♦ —

Jack: I bet your boss was furious when you told him that you would be leaving work next week.

Mack: He certainly was. He thought it was this week.

Customer: Wow. I sure bid a great deal of money for this parrot at the auction. Do you guarantee that he talks?

Auctioneer: I'm positive he does. He's been bidding against you for the last 15 minutes.

— ◆ —

David: Dad, have you ever seen a man-eating tiger?

Ken: No, son. But I have seen a man eating turkey.

— ◆ —

Pam: My cat just took first prize in a bird show.

Melba: How could your cat win first prize at a bird show?

Pam: He ate the prize canary.

— ◆ —

Zack: Would you rather have a lion or a bear eat you?

Larry: I'd rather the lion ate the bear.

— ◆ —

Wife: The doctor told you to take one of these pills three times a day.

Husband: How can I take a pill more than once?

— ◆ —

Amy: Can a match box?

David: No, but a tin can.

Paul: In what kind of home do the buffalo roam?
Kelly: A very dirty one.

— ♦ —

Cathy: Which is better, happiness or a penny?
Nancy: A penny. Nothing is better than happiness...and a penny is better than nothing.

— ♦ —

Did you hear about the man who was driving through the country and saw a hitchhiker who had a rope in his hand? On the end of the rope was a black and white cow.

Driver: I can take you but your cow won't fit into my car.
Hitchhiker: That's no problem. She will follow us by herself.

The hitchhiker got in and the driver stepped on the gas and went to 30 miles an hour. The cow followed behind the car about 50 feet back. The driver went to 50 miles per hour. Somehow the cow was keeping pace about 30 feet behind the car. The driver went to 65 miles per hour. He looked in the rearview mirror and noticed that the cow was running ten feet behind his car with her tongue hanging out of her mouth.

Driver: I'm worried about your cow. Her tongue is hanging out of her mouth to the right.
Hitchhiker: Oh, that's okay. That means she wants to pass you.

Larry: A man went to his office building but found that all the doors and windows were locked, and that he had forgotten his keys. How did he get in?

Jeff: I give up.

Larry: He ran round and round the office building until he was all in.

Olaf & Vito

Olaf: What do they call a crazy pickle?

Vito: I have no clue.

Olaf: A daffydill.

— ◆ —

Olaf: What person can jump higher than a tall building?

Vito: I don't know.

Olaf: Anyone can. Tall buildings don't jump.

— ◆ —

Olaf: What would you get if you crossed an eagle and a skunk?

Vito: Beats me.

Olaf: An animal that stunk to high heaven.

— ◆ —

Olaf: What do you get if you cross a cat and a lemon?

Vito: I can't guess.

Olaf: A sourpuss.

Olaf: What did Cinderella say when her holiday snapshots were late?
Vito: I have no idea.
Olaf: Someday my prints will come.

— ◆ —

Olaf: What is the wasp's favorite television network in England?
Vito: You tell me.
Olaf: The Bee-Bee C.

— ◆ —

Olaf: What is the difference between a tight shoe and an oak tree?
Vito: Who knows?
Olaf: One makes acorns and the other makes corns ache.

— ◆ —

Olaf: What newspaper did the cavemen read?
Vito: My mind is a blank.
Olaf: Prehistoric Times.

— ◆ —

Olaf: What kind of doctor treats ducks?
Vito: That's a mystery.
Olaf: A quack doctor.

Olaf: What will not speak unless it is spoken to and cannot be seen but only heard?

Vito: I'm a blank.

Olaf: An echo.

— ◆ —

Olaf: When a female centipede walks by two male centipedes, what does one male centipede say to the other male centipede?

Vito: I'm in the dark.

Olaf: What a beautiful pair of legs, pair of legs, pair of legs...

— ◆ —

Olaf: What is the difference between the Prince of Wales and a tennis ball?

Vito: I pass.

Olaf: One is heir to the throne and the other is thrown into the air.

What If?

Q: If a man were born in Russia, raised in Brazil, came to America, and died in Dallas, Texas, what is he?

A: Dead.

— ◆ —

Q: If a cow's head is pointing south, where would its tail be pointing?

A: To the ground.

Q: If a telegraph operator from New Mexico married a telephone operator from Nevada, what would they become?

A: A western union.

— ♦ —

Q: If you were swimming in the ocean and a big alligator attacked you, what should you do?

A: Nothing. There are no alligators in the ocean.

— ♦ —

Q: If a band were playing music during a lightning storm, who would be in the most danger of being struck by lightning?

A: The conductor.

— ♦ —

Q: If the green house is on the north, the red house on the south, and the purple house on the east, where is the White House?

A: In Washington, D.C.

— ♦ —

Q: If there are 17 boys and only 6 apples, what is the easiest way to equally divide the apples among the boys?

A. Make applesauce.

Q: If it takes 13 men 11 days to dig a hole, how long will it take 7 men to dig half a hole?

A: There is no such thing as half a hole.

— ◆ —

Q: If a man rides to a farm on Friday and stays four days, how can he ride out on Friday?

A: Friday is the name of his horse.

— ◆ —

Q: If King Kong went to Hong Kong to play Ping-Pong and he died, what would they put on his coffin?

A: A lid.

Gilroy & Oliver

Gilroy: What is the science of shopping called?
Oliver: Who knows?
Gilroy: Buyology.

— ◆ —

Gilroy: What is a bacteria?
Oliver: I can't guess.
Gilroy: The rear entrance of a cafeteria.

— ◆ —

Gilroy: What is the most valuable fish in the water?
Oliver: I have no idea.
Gilroy: Goldfish.

Gilroy: What do you get if you cross sugar and egg whites and a monkey?
Oliver: I don't know.
Gilroy: Meringue Outan.

— ♦ —

Gilroy: What belongs to you, but other people use it more than you do?
Oliver: Beats me.
Gilroy: Your name.

— ♦ —

Gilroy: What did Columbus see on his left hand when he discovered America?
Oliver: You tell me.
Gilroy: His five fingers.

— ♦ —

Gilroy: What was the tallest mountain before Mount Everest was discovered?
Oliver: I give up.
Gilroy: Mount Everest.

— ♦ —

Gilroy: What is green, has bumps, and goes click-click?
Oliver: I have no clue.
Gilroy: A ballpoint pickle.

Gilroy: What do you call a boy named Lee who wants to be by himself all the time?
Oliver: You've got me.
Gilroy: Lonely.

— ◆ —

Gilroy: What kind of table has no legs?
Oliver: My mind is a blank.
Gilroy: A multiplication table.

— ◆ —

Gilroy: What message is recorded the same whether it is from right to left or up or down?
Oliver: I don't know.
Gilroy: SOS.

— ◆ —

Gilroy: What do you call the most unhappy birds in the world?
Oliver: It's unknown to me.
Gilroy: Bluebirds.

— ◆ —

Gilroy: What is worse than a centipede with sore feet?
Oliver: Search me.
Gilroy: A giraffe with a sore throat.

Gilroy: What does a duck wear to a fancy party?
Oliver: I'm in the dark.
Gilroy: A duxedo.

— ♦ —

Gilroy: What did Delaware?
Oliver: I don't have the foggiest.
Gilroy: She wore her New Jersey.

Somebody's at the Door

Knock, knock.
Who's there?
Amana.
Amana who?
Amana very bad mood.

— ♦ —

Knock, knock.
Who's there?
Yule.
Yule who?
Yule never guess.

— ♦ —

Knock, knock.
Who's there?
William Tell.
William Tell who?
William Tell your mother to come to the door.

Knock, knock.
Who's there?
Wednesday.
Wednesday who?
Wednesday saints go marching in...

— ♦ —

Knock, knock.
Who's there?
Who.
Who who?
There's a terrible echo in here, isn't there?

— ♦ —

Knock, knock.
Who's there?
Thistle.
Thistle who?
Thistle will not be the last time I knock on your door.

— ♦ —

Knock, knock.
Who's there?
Lettuce.
Lettuce who?
Lettuce in and we'll tell you another knock-knock joke.

Knock, knock.
Who's there?
Toulouse.
Toulouse who?
Toulouse ten ugly pounds, cut off your head.

— ◆ —

Knock, knock.
Who's there?
Rubber Duck.
Rubber Duck who?
Rubber Duck dub...three men in a tub...

— ◆ —

Knock, knock.
Who's there?
Radio.
Radio who?
Radio not, here I come.

— ◆ —

Knock, knock.
Who's there?
Mandy.
Mandy who?
Mandy lifeboats. I'm drowning.

Knock, knock.
Who's there?
Ken.
Ken who?
Ken I come in? It's very cold out here.

— ◆ —

Knock, knock.
Who's there?
Farley.
Farley who?
Farley the leader.

— ◆ —

Knock, knock.
Who's there?
Enoch.
Enoch who?
Enoch and Enoch but nobody opens the door.

— ◆ —

Knock, knock.
Who's there?
Earl.
Earl who?
Earl be glad to tell you if you open the door.

Knock, knock.
Who's there?
Enoch.
Enoch who?
Enoch and Enoch but nobody opens the door.

Knock, knock.
Who's there?
Ella.
Ella who?
Ella-vator. Doesn't that give you a lift?

— ◆ —

Knock, knock.
Who's there?
Dwayne.
Dwayne who?
Dwayne in Spain falls mainly on the plain.

— ◆ —

Knock, knock.
Who's there?
Dishes.
Dishes who?
Dishes is not the end of my knock-knock jokes.

— ◆ —

Knock, knock.
Who's there?
Dewey.
Dewey who?
Dewey have to keep telling knock-knock jokes?

Igor & Boris

Igor: Did you hear about the riot in the library?
Boris: No, what happened?
Igor: Someone found time bomb in the dictionary.

— ◆ —

Igor: Did you hear about the cat that loved tennis?
Boris: Why?
Igor: He had two brothers in the racket.

— ◆ —

Igor: My brother is so strong that he can rip a telephone book in half.
Boris: That's nothing. My mother rushed out the door this morning, got in the car, and tore up the street.

— ◆ —

Igor: Don't be afraid. This dog will eat off your hand.
Boris: That's what I'm afraid of.

— ◆ —

Igor: Do the Smokey the Bear posters really help?
Boris: They sure do. Since they have put up the posters there hasn't been a single forest fire in Brooklyn.

Igor: My wife is black and blue because she puts on cold cream, face cream, wrinkle cream, vanishing cream, hand cream, and skin cream every night.

Boris: Why should that make her black and blue?

Igor: She keeps slipping out of bed.

— ◆ —

Igor: Did you hear the story about the man who lives on nothing but garlic alone?

Boris: No. But any man who lives on garlic, should live alone.

— ◆ —

Igor: Did you hear what the termite said when he walked into the saloon?

Boris: No, I didn't.

Igor: He said, "Is the bar tender here?"

— ◆ —

Igor: Two fathers and two sons went duck hunting. Each shot a duck and they shot only three ducks in all. How come?

Boris: Probably because the hunters were a man, his son, and his grandson.

— ◆ —

Igor: Did you hear in the news about the turtle on the Los Angeles Freeway?

Boris: What was a turtle doing on the freeway?

Igor: About one mile an hour.

Igor: On my farm we go to bed with the chickens.
Boris: I'd rather sleep in my own bed.

— ◆ —

Igor: I went to the doctor about my poor memory.
Boris: What did he do?
Igor: He made me pay in advance.

— ◆ —

Igor: Every day my dog and I go for a tramp in the park.
Boris: Does your dog enjoy it?
Igor: Oh, yes. But the tramp is getting fed up with it.

— ◆ —

Igor: When I was younger, everyone called me wonderboy.
Boris: One look at you and I would wonder, too.

— ◆ —

Igor: I have traced my ancestors and found out that I am a descendant of a king.
Boris: Yeah. King Kong.

— ◆ —

Igor: Does your wife cook by electricity or gas?
Boris: I really don't know. I've never tried to cook her.

Igor: The zoo manager told me that your son is in trouble for feeding the monkeys.

Boris: What's wrong with that? People do that all the time.

Igor: He fed them to the lions.

— ◆ —

Igor: Where do you bathe?
Boris: In the spring.
Igor: I said where, not when.

The Answer Man

Q: Why do plumbers wear yellow suspenders?
A: To keep their pants up.

— ◆ —

Q: Why is it dangerous to put grease on your hair?
A: Because everything would slip your mind.

— ◆ —

Q: Why do flies walk on the ceiling?
A: Because if they walked on the floor, someone might step on them.

— ◆ —

Q: Why do bees hum?
A: Because they don't remember the words to the song.

Q: Why do they always put blue clothes on baby boys and pink clothes on baby girls?
A: Because they can't dress themselves.

— ♦ —

Q: Why should you never mention the number 288 in front of your math teacher?
A: Because it is two gross. (A gross is 144—get it?)

— ♦ —

Q: Why does time fly?
A: To escape from people who are trying to kill it.

— ♦ —

Q: Why do women use curlers at night when they do not have an alarm clock?
A: So they can wake up curly in the morning.

— ♦ —

Q: Why does that weird man take a bale of hay to bed with him?
A: To feed his nightmares.

— ♦ —

Q: Why do teachers think they are so special?
A: Because they think they are in a class of their own.

Q: Why do skunks argue all the time?
A: Because they like to raise a stink.

— ◆ —

Q: Why did the Boy Scout get so dizzy?
A: He did too many good turns.

— ◆ —

Q: Why do hurricanes travel so fast?
A: If they traveled slowly, we would have to call them slow-i-canes.

— ◆ —

Q: Why did the kangaroo cross the road?
A: It was the chicken's day off.

— ◆ —

Q: Why is honey so scarce in Boston?
A: Because there is only one B in Boston.

— ◆ —

Q: Why did the one-handed man cross the road?
A: To get to the secondhand shop.

— ◆ —

Q: Why is the letter D like a bad boy?
A: Both make ma mad.

Q: Why do white sheep eat more grass than black sheep?

A: Because there are more of them.

Petula & Zelda

Petula: Why did you paint your car brown on one side and blue on the other side?

Zelda: So that if I ever run into anyone else's car, the witnesses will have conflicting stories if I have to go to court.

— ◆ —

Petula: What do frogs wear to the beach?

Zelda: I have no clue.

Petula: Open-toad sandals.

— ◆ —

Petula: What do they call a cow that works for a gardener?

Zelda: I don't know.

Petula: A lawn mooer.

— ◆ —

Petula: What loses its head every day but gets it back at night?

Zelda: Beats me.

Petula: A pillow.

Petula: What is the best way to see flying saucers?
Zelda: I can't guess.
Petula: Get mad at your husband.

— ♦ —

Petula: What causes the most noise in space?
Zelda: I have no idea.
Petula: Shooting stars.

— ♦ —

Petula: What do you get when you cross a trumpet and a flute?
Zelda: You tell me.
Petula: A tootie flooty.

— ♦ —

Petula: What happened to the woman who covered herself with vanishing cream?
Zelda: I give up.
Petula: Nobody knows.

— ♦ —

Petula: What is the difference between a toothpick and a sword?
Zelda: Who knows?
Petula: Well, if you don't know, you'd better not pick your teeth.

Petula: What is purple and divides the United States from Canada?

Zelda: You've got me.

Petula: The Grape Lakes.

— ♦ —

Petula: Which would you rather be, half-drowned or saved?

Zelda: Saved of course.

Petula: But if you are only half-drowned you are saved.

— ♦ —

Petula: What do you get if you cross a skunk and an owl that can't speak?

Zelda: My mind is a blank.

Petula: An animal that smells bad and doesn't give a hoot.

— ♦ —

Petula: What lives in the sea, has eight legs, and is quick on the draw?

Zelda: I don't have the foggiest.

Petula: Billy the Squid.

— ♦ —

Petula: What did one big toe say to the other big toe?

Zelda: Search me.

Petula: Don't look now but there's a couple of big heels following us.

Petula: What would happen if you cut your left side off?

Zelda: You'd be all right.

— ◆ —

Petula: What is the best thing to do when you don't feel well?

Zelda: I pass.

Petula: Take off your gloves.

— ◆ —

Petula: What did the painter say to the wall?

Zelda: I don't know.

Petula: One more crack like that and I'll plaster you.

Use the Doorbell

Knock, knock.

Who's there?

Deluxe.

Deluxe who?

Deluxe Ness Monster.

— ◆ —

Knock, knock.

Who's there?

Celia.

Celia who?

Celia later, alligator.

Knock, knock.
Who's there?
Caesar.
Caesar who?
Caesar jolly good fellow...

— ♦ —

Knock, knock.
Who's there?
Canoe.
Canoe who?
Canoe please get off my foot?

— ♦ —

Knock, knock.
Who's there?
Barbie.
Barbie who?
Barbie Q. Chicken.

— ♦ —

Knock, knock.
Who's there?
Britches.
Britches who?
London Britches falling down...

Knock, knock.
Who's there?
Avenue.
Avenue who?
Avenue been missing me?

— ◆ —

Knock, knock.
Who's there?
Archer.
Archer who?
Archer glad to see me?

— ◆ —

Knock, knock.
Who's there?
Aldous.
Aldous who?
Aldous knocking gives me a headache.

— ◆ —

Knock, knock.
Who's there?
Abbey.
Abbey who?
Abbey birthday to you.

Knock, knock.
Who's there?
Aiken.
Aiken who?
Oh, my Aiken back.

— ◆ —

Knock, knock.
Who's there?
Eiffel.
Eiffel who?
Eiffel off the step and hurt my foot.

— ◆ —

Knock, knock.
Who's there?
Datsun.
Datsun who?
Datsun awful knock-knock joke.

— ◆ —

Knock, knock.
Who's there?
Midas.
Midas who?
Midas well open the door.

Knock, knock.
Who's there?
Oscar and Greta.
Oscar and Greta who?
Oscar foolish question, Greta foolish answer.

Ichabod & Ignatius

Ichabod: What did the envelope say when you licked it?
Ignatius: I have no clue.
Ichabod: Nothing. It just shut up.

— ◆ —

Ichabod: What is the best thing for an elk with indigestion?
Ignatius: I don't know.
Ichabod: Elk-A-Seltzer.

— ◆ —

Ichabod: What do you get when you cross a horse and a cow?
Ignatius: I can't guess.
Ichabod: Winnie the Moo.

— ◆ —

Ichabod: What goes in one ear and out the other?
Ignatius: I have no idea.
Ichabod: A worm in a corn field.

Ichabod: What do people in Tibet call small black cats?
Ignatius: Beats me.
Ichabod: Kittens.

— ◆ —

Ichabod: What does the hangman like to read?
Ignatius: You tell me.
Ichabod: The noosepaper.

— ◆ —

Ichabod: What is the whitest part of a baseball park?
Ignatius: I give up.
Ichabod: The bleachers.

— ◆ —

Ichabod: What can never be made right?
Ignatius: Who knows?
Ichabod: Your left foot.

— ◆ —

Ichabod: What is always behind the time?
Ignatius: You've got me.
Ichabod: The back of a clock.

— ◆ —

Ichabod: What is the fastest fish in the water?
Ignatius: That's a mystery.
Ichabod: Motorpike.

Ichabod: What do you get when you cross a crocodile with an abalone?

Ignatius: My mind is a blank.

Ichabod: A crocabalone.

— ◆ —

Ichabod: What is the favorite breakfast food of cats?

Ignatius: I'm a blank.

Ichabod: Mice Crispies.

— ◆ —

Ichabod: What do you call a tomato that insults a farmer?

Ignatius: I don't have the foggiest.

Ichabod: A very fresh vegetable.

— ◆ —

Ichabod: What is five Q and five Q?

Ignatius: Ten Q.

Ichabod: You're welcome.

— ◆ —

Ichabod: What is sweet, comes in different flavors and colors, and makes music?

Ignatius: Search me.

Ichabod: Cello pudding.

Ichabod: What happens when you tell jokes about the stomach?
Ignatius: You get belly laughs.

— ◆ —

Ichabod: What is served but never eaten?
Ignatius: I pass.
Ichabod: A volleyball.

Did Your Tang Get Toungled Up?

Say the following phrases three times...real fast.

A capable cook cooked cupcakes in a cook's cap.

— ◆ —

The gray ghost goes by Barney Booth's Blue Goose bus.

— ◆ —

The silent shark ate sheep in the cheap sheep soup shop.

— ◆ —

Billy Blob's big blue blister burst.

— ◆ —

King Kong Carl coops up crying cute cooks.

Shy sly slim Sheriff Shultz slays seven sly shy slithering snakes.

— ◆ —

Charlie Chisim chomps cheap charcoal cherries.

— ◆ —

Six sick sad snakes slip and slide off slick ski slopes.

— ◆ —

Betty Bliss blended blue-black blueberries in the blender.

— ◆ —

Sixty-six shy sick sticky snakes slithered silently.

— ◆ —

Which wretched witches watch Wills Walrus washing wet watches while willingly waiting with Wanda Whale?

Leftovers

Larry: I have to go now, Jeff. Could you come outside with me and help me check out the taillights on my car? I don't know if they are working.

Jeff: Okay.

Larry: I turned them on. Are they blinking?

Jeff: No...yes...no...yes...no...yes...

Shy sly slim Sheriff Shultz slays seven sly shy slithering snakes.

In the park a man sat down on a bench and started eating his hot dog and french fries. It wasn't long before a lady came along with a small dog who was very much interested in what the man was eating.

The dog kept jumping on the man and yelping.

"Excuse me, madam," said the man. "Do you mind if I toss your dog a bit?"

"Not at all," replied the woman.

So the man picked up her dog and threw it over the wall next to the bench.

— ♦ —

Jeff: How do you like the way I can play the clarinet?

Larry: Frankly, I've heard better sounds coming from a leaking balloon.

— ♦ —

Jeff: Well then, if you don't like the sounds of my clarinet, how do you like my singing?

Larry: I wouldn't say your voice was out of this world. But it is certainly unearthly.

— ♦ —

Jeff: Okay, you don't like my clarinet or my singing. How about my swimming? I have been swimming since I was five years old.

Larry: You must really be tired.

Jeff: Oh, Larry, before you leave...Guess what I just bought?

Larry: What's that?

Jeff: A man came to the door and sold me the Nile River.

Larry: Egypt you.

— ◆ —

Jeff: I have to go to the hospital later. What is the fastest way to get there?

Larry: Stand in the middle of the road.

— ◆ —

Jeff: Oh, by the way, Larry, next week I am going to go to New York.

Larry: Are you going to go by Buffalo?

Jeff: Don't be silly. I am going to go by train.

— ◆ —

Larry: Well, Jeff, when you get to New York, you should take a cruise of New York Harbor.

Jeff: How fast does the boat go?

Larry: About 20 knots an hour.

Jeff: Wow! How long does it take to untie the knots?

— ◆ —

Larry: While you are near New York Harbor, Jeff, watch out for the duck-doo.

Jeff: What's duck-doo?

Larry: It goes "Quack-quack."

Jeff: Someone said that they have good chicken soup in New York. Is chicken soup good for your health?

Larry: Not if you're a chicken.

— ◆ —

Larry: By the way, Jeff, how did you get that lump on your head?

Jeff: I got hit by some beans.

Larry: How could tiny little beans give you such a big lump?

Jeff: They were still in the can.

— ◆ —

Mother: Gerald, I am so proud of you. You received all sorts of awards while you were at summer camp. Here's one for sailing, one for bow and arrows, and one for horseback riding. What is this gold medal for?

Gerald: For being the first one to have my trunk packed neatly to go home.

Mother: That's great! How did you do it so quickly?

Gerald: I never unpacked.

— ◆ —

Harley: Why are you putting two quarters under your pillow?

Charlie: These are my sleeping quarters.

— ◆ —

Sign on the back of a garbage truck: Satisfaction guaranteed or double your garbage back.

Boyfriend: Honey, here are some sweets for the sweet.

Girlfriend: Thank you very much. Won't you have some of these nuts?

— ◆ —

Juliet: Romeo, O Romeo, wherefore art thou, Romeo?

Romeo: Down here in the flowers. The trellis broke.

— ◆ —

Cityslicker: Why do bears live in caves?

Hunter: Because they can't afford apartments in the city.

— ◆ —

P.K.: How do you make a banana shake?

Kelley: Take it to a scary movie.

— ◆ —

Melba: Swimming is one of the best exercises for keeping slim.

Pam: Did you ever see a sea lion?

Ruby & Pearl

Ruby: What rock group is famous for killing thousands of germs?

Pearl: I don't know.

Ruby: The Bleach Boys.

Ruby: What would you do if a hippopotamus sat in front of you at the movies?
Pearl: Miss most of the movie.

— ♦ —

Ruby: What happened to Ray when he was stepped on by a hippopotamus?
Pearl: Beats me.
Ruby: He became an X-Ray.

— ♦ —

Ruby: What is the difference between a hill and a pill?
Pearl: I can't guess.
Ruby: One goes up and the other goes down.

— ♦ —

Ruby: What is the difference between a girl and a postage stamp?
Pearl: I have no idea.
Ruby: One is a mail fee and the other is a female.

— ♦ —

Ruby: Just after the earthquake, what did one mountain say to the other mountain?
Pearl: You tell me.
Ruby: It's not my fault.

Ruby: What is green, has big eyes, and makes a loud noise?
Pearl: I give up.
Ruby: A frog horn.

— ♦ —

Ruby: What is the best way to raise a hippopotamus?
Pearl: Who knows?
Ruby: With a crane.

— ♦ —

Ruby: When a frog has a car that breaks down, what does he do?
Pearl: You've got me.
Ruby: He calls a toad truck.

— ♦ —

Ruby: What plays the piano and works for Chicken of the Sea?
Pearl: That's a mystery.
Ruby: Piano-tuna.

— ♦ —

Ruby: What is the smallest bridge in the world?
Pearl: I'm a blank.
Ruby: The bridge of your nose.

Ruby: What do you call someone who steals Farmer John's pigs?

Pearl: Search me.

Ruby: A ham-burglar.

— ♦ —

Ruby: What is small, green, and is a Kung Fu expert?

Pearl: I pass.

Ruby: Bruce Pea.

— ♦ —

Ruby: What will be the last thing said on the Last Day?

Pearl: I don't know.

Ruby: Armageddon out of here.

— ♦ —

Ruby: What clothes do lawyers wear in court?

Pearl: I give up.

Ruby: Lawsuits.

Are You Still There?

Knock, knock.

Who's there?

Little old lady.

Little old lady who?

I didn't know you could yodel.

Knock, knock.
Who's there?
Amanda.
Amanda who?
Amanda fix your washing machine.

— ◆ —

Knock, knock.
Who's there?
Waiter.
Waiter who?
Waiter minute while I tie my shoe.

— ◆ —

Knock, knock.
Who's there?
Stan.
Stan who?
Stan back, quick, I think I'm going to be sick.

— ◆ —

Knock, knock.
Who's there?
Norma Lee.
Norma Lee who?
Norma Lee I don't go around knocking on doors.

Knock, knock.
Who's there?
Myth.
Myth who?
I Myth you, too.

— ♦ —

Knock, knock.
Who's there?
Midas.
Midas who?
Midas well relax. I'm not going away.

— ♦ —

Knock, knock.
Who's there?
Minerva.
Minerva who?
Minerva-s wreck from all these questions.

— ♦ —

Knock, knock.
Who's there?
Red.
Red who?
Red peppers. Isn't that a hot one?

Knock, knock.
Who's there?
Armenia.
Armenia who?
Armenia every word I say.

— ◆ —

Knock, knock.
Who's there?
Samoa.
Samoa who?
Samoa old friends from high school.

— ◆ —

Knock, knock.
Who's there?
Aida.
Aida who?
Aida lot of ice cream and my stomach hurts.

— ◆ —

Knock, knock.
Who's there?
Agatha.
Agatha who?
Agatha headache. Do you have any aspirin?

Knock, knock.
Who's there?
Adolf.
Adolf who?
Adolf ball hit me in the mowf.

Archibald & Percival

Archibald: What roof covers the noisiest tenant?
Percival: I have no clue.
Archibald: The roof of your mouth.

— ♦ —

Archibald: What do you get when you cross hot rolls from the oven with a comedian who is angry?
Percival: I don't know.
Archibald: Hot cross puns.

— ♦ —

Archibald: What kind of person cannot get enough cocoa?
Percival: I can't guess.
Archibald: A coconut.

— ♦ —

Archibald: What type of pigeon is caught sitting down a lot?
Percival: Who knows?
Archibald: A stool pigeon.

Archibald: What kind of cookie breaks easily?
Percival: Beats me.
Archibald: Gingersnaps.

— ◆ —

Archibald: What did the dirt say to the rain?
Percival: I have no idea.
Archibald: If this keeps up, my name will be mud.

— ◆ —

Archibald: What is the shortest month in a year?
Percival: You tell me.
Archibald: May. It only has three letters.

— ◆ —

Archibald: What is the most talkative of the animals?
Percival: You've got me.
Archibald: The yak.

— ◆ —

Archibald: What game do mice love to play?
Percival: I'm in the dark.
Archibald: Hide and squeak.

— ◆ —

Archibald: What did the banana say to the monkey?
Percival: I don't have the foggiest.
Archibald: Nothing. Bananas don't talk.

Archibald: What is yellow, soft, full of cheese, and goes around and around?

Percival: It's unknown to me.

Archibald: A long-playing omelette.

— ◆ —

Archibald: If you cross a germ with a comedian, what do you get?

Percival: My mind is a blank.

Archibald: A lot of sick jokes.

— ◆ —

Archibald: What is the difference between a clumsy outfielder and a rain gutter?

Percival: I don't know.

Archibald: One catches drops and the other drops catches.

The Answer Man

Q: Why did Jack and Jill roll down the hill?

A: They got tired of walking.

— ◆ —

Q: Why does underwear last longer than all other clothing?

A: Because it's never worn out.

Q: Why did the man go crazy in the shoe store?
A: He was told that it was a good place for a fit.

— ◆ —

Q: Why should you never tell pigs any of your secrets?
A: They're squealers.

— ◆ —

Q: What makes Frosty the Snowman so popular?
A: He's cool.

— ◆ —

Q: Why are storytellers very strange?
A: Because tales come out of their heads.

— ◆ —

Q: Why did Robin Hood steal from the wealthy?
A: The poor didn't have any money.

— ◆ —

Q: Why couldn't Batman go fishing?
A: Robin ate all the worms.

— ◆ —

Q: Why did the horse cough and sneeze?
A: Because it had a little colt.

Q: Why does your hand get tired after writing with a pencil for a long time?

A: Because the pencil is full of lead.

— ♦ —

Q: Why is it dangerous to tell any secrets around a clock?

A: Because time will tell.

— ♦ —

Q: Why did all the king's horses and all the king's men have such a difficult time putting Humpty Dumpty back together again?

A: Because he wasn't everything he was cracked up to be.

— ♦ —

Q: Why is it impossible to rain for two nights in a row?

A: Because there is a day between.

— ♦ —

Q: Why was the Egyptian boy so confused?

A: Because his daddy was a mummy.

— ♦ —

Q: Why did the tailor's son have such a bad name?

A: Because he was the son of a sew-and-sew.

Q: Why did the cow jump over the moon?
A: The farmer's hands were cold.

— ◆ —

Q: Why do horses live in barns?
A: Because they are too large for birdhouses.

— ◆ —

Q: Why did the dinosaur cross the road?
A: Because they didn't have chickens in those days.

Dixie & Dottie

Dixie: Why is your brother so small?
Dottie: I don't know.
Dixie: He's your half brother.

— ◆ —

Dixie: What goes "Dot-dot-dot, dash-dash-dash, dot-dot-dot?"
Dottie: I have no clue.
Dixie: Morse Toad.

— ◆ —

Dixie: What did the football team do when they drank up all the Coke in the United States?
Dottie: I can't guess.
Dixie: They drank Canada Dry.

Dixie: What do they call a very fat tree limb?
Dottie: Beats me.
Dixie: Porky Twig.

— ◆ —

Dixie: What are pants with a rip in them called?
Dottie: I have no idea.
Dixie: Van Winkle trousers.

— ◆ —

Dixie: What do you get if you cross an old clock with a chicken?
Dottie: You tell me.
Dixie: A grandfather cluck.

— ◆ —

Dixie: What chicken was a famous American patriot?
Dottie: I give up.
Dixie: Pat-chick Henry.

— ◆ —

Dixie: What do you call it when it rains chickens, ducks, and turkeys?
Dottie: Who knows?
Dixie: Fowl weather.

— ◆ —

Dixie: What is green and goes round and around?
Dottie: A pickle in a clothes dryer.

Dixie: What should you say if you are swimming in the ocean and happen to get entangled in kelp?
Dottie: My mind is a blank.
Dixie: KELP!

— ◆ —

Dixie: What do you get if you cross a hippopotamus and a blackbird?
Dottie: I don't have the foggiest.
Dixie: Lots of broken telephone poles.

— ◆ —

Dixie: What is fat, ugly, hairy, and makes animals yawn?
Dottie: It's unknown to me.
Dixie: A wild bore.

— ◆ —

Dixie: What should you do to keep from getting seasick?
Dottie: I'm in the dark.
Dixie: Bolt your food down.

— ◆ —

Dixie: What is the fastest way to find a needle in a rug?
Dottie: How should I know?
Dixie: Walk around in your bare feet.

Dixie: What do you call a crazy blackbird?
Dottie: Search me.
Dixie: A raven lunatic.

— ♦ —

Dixie: What did the beaver say to the aspen tree?
Dottie: I pass.
Dixie: It's been nice gnawing you.

— ♦ —

Dixie: What happened when the hyena swallowed a
bouillon cube?
Dottie: I don't know.
Dixie: He made a laughing stock of himself.

Stop All That Knocking!

Knock, knock.
Who's there?
Darren.
Darren who?
Darren young man on the flying trapeze.

— ♦ —

Knock, knock.
Who's there?
Candy.
Candy who?
Candy cow jump over the moon?

Knock, knock.
Who's there?
Candy.
Candy who?
Candy cow jump over the moon?

Knock, knock.
Who's there?
Darius.
Darius who?
Darius a lot of things I need to tell you.

— ◆ —

Knock, knock.
Who's there?
Joe King.
Joe King who?
You must be Joe King.

— ◆ —

Knock, knock.
Who's there?
Butcher.
Butcher who?
Butcher money where your mouth is.

— ◆ —

Knock, knock.
Who's there?
Atlas.
Atlas who?
Atlas it's Friday and there is no school tomorrow.

Knock, knock.
Who's there?
Burton.
Burton who?
Burton the hand is worth two in the bush.

— ◆ —

Knock, knock.
Who's there?
Athena.
Athena who?
Athena flying saucer.

— ◆ —

Knock, knock.
Who's there?
Aunt Lou.
Aunt Lou who?
Aunt Lou do you think you are?

— ◆ —

Knock, knock.
Who's there?
Cheer.
Cheer who?
Cheer up, this is the last knock-knock joke.

Other Books by Bob Phillips

- *World's Greatest Collection of Clean Jokes*
- *More Good Clean Jokes*
- *The Last of the Good Clean Jokes*
- *The Return of the Good Clean Jokes*
- *The All American Joke Book*
- *The World's Greatest Collection of Heavenly Humor*
- *The Best of the Good Clean Jokes*
- *The Best of the Good Clean Jokes Perpetual Calendar*
- *Wit and Wisdom*
- *Humor Is Tremendous*
- *The All-New Clean Joke Book*
- *Good Clean Jokes for Kids*
- *Bob Phillips' The Encyclopedia of Good Clean Jokes*
- *Ultimate Good Clean Jokes for Kids*
- *Awesome Good Clean Jokes for Kids*
- *Wacky Good Clean Jokes for Kids*
- *Loony Good Clean Jokes for Kids*
- *Bible Brainteasers*
- *The Ultimate Bible Trivia Challenge*
- *The Little Book of Bible Trivia*
- *How Can I Be Sure? A Pre-Marriage Inventory*
- *Anger Is a Choice*
- *Redi-Reference*
- *Redi-Reference Daily Bible Reading Plan*
- *The Delicate Art of Dancing with Porcupines*
- *God's Hand Over Hume*
- *Praise Is a Three-Lettered Word—Joy*
- *The Handbook for Headache Relief*
- *Friendship, Love & Laughter*